LIFE Foundation Publications
Maristowe House
Dover Street
Bilston
West Midlands WV14 6AL
UK

Original design: Regina Doerstel
Graphic design and typesetting: Jane Clapham
Printed by Redwood Books, Kennet Way, Trowbridge, Wiltshire
Cover photograph courtesy of the Telegraph Colour Library

ISBN 1 873606 04 4

Your Personal

PEACE
FORMULA

FOR A
NEW MILLENNIUM

Dr Mansukh Patel

The Peace Formula

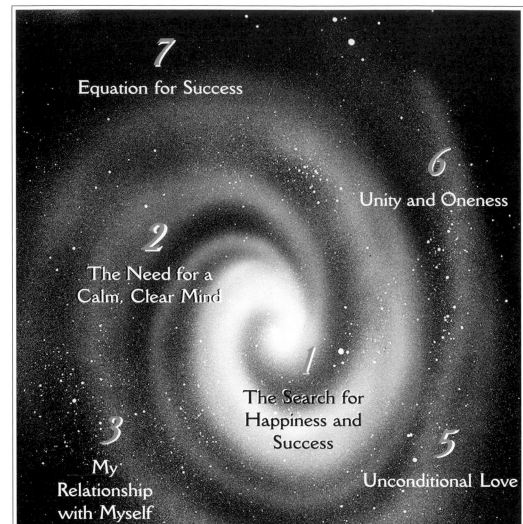

I dedicate this book to the person
who is the greatest source of inspiration
in your life

CONTENTS

6 Unity and Oneness

7 Equation for Success

FOREWORD

It has been such a great privilege and joy to have known and worked with Mansukh for many years and to share his vision for a world where people are at peace with themselves and each other. There is no one I know who is more qualified to guide and direct people towards this state of inner contentment, simply because of the way he is himself.

Mahatma Gandhi once said, 'My life is my message,' and this is also true of Mansukh, whose dynamic personality and simple lifestyle make him a living example of what he teaches. I remember so many incidents that illustrate this on our Eurowalk tours, but one that stands out more than most is watching him playing football with a group of refugee children in Bosnia. He left the laughter and excitement of the game to go to a small child he had noticed crouching by a tree and crying. Within minutes, the pain on that child's face was starting to dissolve, together with the unspoken question, 'Shall I trust again?' Then it was my turn to cry. Wherever there is a call, whether from thousands or just one individual, Mansukh cannot help but respond.

Mahatma Gandhi has always been one of the greatest inspirations in Mansukh's life. It was Gandhi, together with his father, who inspired him to start his well-known peace walks which have earned him the title of 'The Young Gandhi' in Belgium and the Netherlands. On his most recent walk he led nearly a thousand people through the streets of Rotterdam as part of the World Peace - Inner Peace Conference. He carried the Peace Flame which had touched the pain and suffering of Sarejevo and Mostar, Red Square and borderlands of Chechnya, Northern Ireland and the camps of Auschwitz and Birkenau and, followed by those thousand people, entered St Laurens Church, to light the touchpaper of the joy of humanity.

Mansukh's vision for a peaceful world encompasses his dream to create a future in which young people can grow up in peace and security, where they are able to freely express and live out their own dreams and visions. These aims have been passionately endorsed by Robert Muller who has offered his own dream for a new millenium as a dedication for this book. I once witnessed Robert's response to a young person who asked him what young people could do for peace. He sank back into himself for a moment and then, with tears rolling down his face, he held up his hands, shaking his head with great feeling and implored him, 'For

1

God's sake, do *something*. Just do *something*!' His response was passionate and alive. And when two people of such passion and vision come together as did Mansukh and Robert at St Laurens Church, where over 1,500 people eventually gathered to celebrate their commitment to peace and the unity of religions, their strength becomes very evident. It acts as a clear signpost for others to follow.

Mansukh's Peace Formula is compiled from all the ideas and techniques that have made him the peacemaker he is. It is simple, clear and direct. It leaves you in no doubt that it is possible for you to re-orientate your life in a peaceful way and discover the truth and strength that are already a part of you. As he has said so many times, 'Peace is here. It is within our grasp.' And in this book, he clearly shows us how to make it a living reality.

Savitri McCuish
Eurowalk team leader
Director of Life Foundation International

MY DREAM 2000

I dream
that on 1 January 2000
The whole world will stand still
In prayer, awe and gratitude
For our beautiful, heavenly Earth
And for the miracle of human life.

I dream
That young and old, rich and poor,
Black and white,
People from North and South,
From East and West,
From all beliefs and cultures
Will join their hands, minds and hearts
in an unprecedented, universal
Bimillennium Celebration of Life.

I dream
That during the year 2000
Innumerable celebrations and events
Will take place all over the globe
To guage the long road covered by
humanity
To study our mistakes
And to plan the feats
Still to be accomplished
For the full flowering of the human
race
In peace, justice and happiness.

I dream
That the few remaining years
To the Bimillennium
Be devoted by all humans, nations
and institutions
To unparallelled thinking, action,
Inspiration, elevations,
Determination and love
To solve our remaining problems
and to achieve
A peaceful, united human family
on Earth.

I dream
That the year 2000
Will be declared World Year of
Thanksgiving
by the United Nations.

I dream
That the third millennium
Will be declared
And made
Humanity's First Millennium of
Peace.

Dr Robert Muller
Chancellor Emeritus, University for Peace
Former Secretary General of the UN

Eurowalk 2000, Life International Conference

FWF AND EUROWALK 2000

January 1992 saw the birth of a global project with a difference. A team of people from the Life Foundation began a journey which was to span thirty-one countries and last eighteen months. The project was named **Friendship Without Frontiers (FWF).**

FWF endeavoured to support local intitiatives and also meet personal needs, building a network of 'caring-in-action' amongst the 'unseen heroes' of the world. So often these brave people go unnoticed and their creative pioneering work is left unsupported. **FWF** aimed to help these people realise they are not alone in their endeavours and that there are other, like-minded groups working all over the world in similar ways. FWF has worked to bring all the groups they have met together, networking them into an amazing tapestry.

FWF has now evolved into **Eurowalk 2000** - the international walking initiative that has travelled the length and breadth of Europe focusing on war zones such as Bosnia, the West Bank, the Sudan, Northern Ireland, and the Chechen borderland in Russia.

Eurowalk 2000 consists of a dedicated team of health professionals and therapists whose aim is to bring hope, humanitarian aid and transformation on every level into the lives of those who need help most. We have assisted UN doctors and NGO aid workers, political and spiritual leaders, paramilitary strategists as well as traumatised refugees.

We have shaken the hands of some and held the hands of others. We have discussed ways forward with political and spiritual leaders and taught self-help techniques to refugees and UN therapists to enable them to endure some of the most stressful circumstances any human being can encounter.

And we have been rewarded beyond any wealth by those special moments in which we have seen the light of hope coming back into the dull, lifeless eyes of a broken-hearted refugee child, or watched a paramilitary leader shed years of political dogma to reveal a heart desperate for peace.

The Peace Formula is a tribute to all the people we have met on our FWF and Eurowalk journeys. It is a seven-point plan for inner ecology, which means creating an environment which starts from within yourself, uplifting the world around you rather than polluting it. The key to peace is to discover that peace already lies within. This means having enough faith in yourself to allow the very best within you to be uncovered.

When life presents challenges that disturb your peace of mind, leaving you feeling helpless and powerless, what can you do? When you feel lonely, what can you do to re-connect with the oneness of life, to feel unified with your fellow human beings? How can you empower yourself to become the successful, contented person you long to be?

The Peace Formula offers practical answers - a guide to work with in your daily life to help you promote inner contentment and fulfilment. It is a simple formula, containing profound insights and a wealth of wisdom, that embraces the laws that govern our universe.

HOW THE PEACE FORMULA CAME ABOUT

It was in November of 1992 I remember, while I was sitting in the Ramakrishna Centre in Calcutta on the far eastern side of India, that the feeling for a peace formula first came to me.

Swami Vivekananda,* like Gandhi, has always been a great font of inspiration in my life. He was known in his time as 'The Lion's Roar of India' and his message has influenced, inspired and transformed hundreds of lives over the last century as a result of his passionate desire to help humanity awaken to the truth. He once said, 'I will inspire men everywhere until the world knows it is one with God' - and everything he did was filled with the conviction of this promise.

It was with these thoughts and the inspiration of Swami Vivekananda all around me, that I looked out of the window of my room and noticed a young man sitting upright on a bicycle. He was gliding along holding a little white dog in one hand while the other held the handlebars with which he skilfully negotiated the chaotic traffic of Calcutta. And I mean chaotic. It was a beautiful sight and spoke to me of the harmony and unity that exists within the chaos of life today. Scenes like this make us realise that there simply must be a God, just for people to be able to survive intact every day!

But what a contrast to the life I had known as a child! And that kind of life still does exist in many parts of India. If you were to go to the little village in Gujerat where my mother was born, for instance, you would witness a very different pace of life, where the rushing fever has not taken over the hearts and minds of the people.

Everywhere you look you see images of contentment and harmonious activity. Many times I have seen hay carts being drawn by camels with big floppy faces and feet. They lollop along so slowly and peacefully that the farmers are able just to sink back against their huge hay-stacks and go to sleep! They have no anxiety about when they will reach their destination and total confidence that the camel will get there eventually.

Such images of contentment can conjure up a feeling of exhilaration inside us because we recognise that we are longing to experience that kind of harmony with life. There is a distinct absence of the stressful uncertainty and the consequent insecurity that prevails in our modern world where

*Ramakrishna's most inspiring disciple

everyone seems to have become obsessed with trying to control and manipulate events.

Contentment will arise quite naturally when we can allow life to take its own course and trust that everything will work out perfectly - just as the farmer trusts his camel to get him where he needs to go. But in the hectic, fast-moving city, living where the rushing fever has reached epidemic proportions, madness is corrupting our lives and contentment is nowhere to be seen.

'Where is humanity rushing to?' I asked myself. 'And how can people be stopped from engaging in so much random activity that is going absolutely nowhere?' The whole emphasis of life has become one of doing and achieving as though we are only here on earth as task completers. People are lost, confused and bewildered as a result of basing their feeling of achievement on external objectives. This attitude simply will not grant inner peace or self-fulfilment. Wealth and fame offer a degree of happiness and contentment, but if they are not based on inner joy, there can never be true satisfaction in any of these achievements. And as we frantically rush towards the new millennium what can we possibly hope to achieve? The only outcome will be events such as Hiroshima - the tragic evidence of man's disconnection from himself and all of life around him.

How can we change the direction that humanity is taking? How can we make this new millenium the greatest time of inspiration and hope?

These were the questions that were burning inside me as I got up to walk to the inner courtyard of the Centre. I was feeling so strongly that the messages and guidelines of truth that had been laid out by such spiritual giants as Gandhi and Vivekananda must not be lost in the dusty annals of time. We simply have to do everything within our power to preserve and carry on their vision and to bring it to the attention of the world.

Each of these giants had come to turn the wheel of dharma and now I felt it was time for me to pick up the wheel and turn it myself. I knew I would have to take the deepest spiritual laws and put them into a form that was easily accessible for all people from every walk of life.

And so, as the waters of the courtyard fountain played gently with the evening sunlight, *The Peace Formula* was conceived inside me. I offer it to you in the sincere hope that it will re-awaken the peace that lies within your own heart.

Mansukh

8

'My crown is in my heart, not on my head;
not decked with diamonds and Indian stones, not to be seen.
My crown is called content;
a crown it is that seldom kings enjoy.'

William Shakespeare, Henry VI Part III

THE SEARCH FOR HAPPINESS AND SUCCESS

the wanting mind

THE WANTING MIND

What is the nature of our search for happiness and success? Have you ever asked yourself why you are doing what you are doing? Why are you in your job? Why do you want to make money? Why do you want to provide for your family?

I think you will agree that everything we do in life is to seek happiness. In fact, life has become a constant and never-ending pursuit of a feeling of contentment and peace both within ourselves and with life itself.

As I have travelled around the globe, I have found that regardless of country, culture or creed, every person, everywhere, is yearning for the very same thing - and that is a simple feeling of inner contentment.

the answer lies within
There is a deer that produces musk in its own body. When it begins to smell the musk, it roams endlessly through the forest searching for the source of this exquisite aroma. It is totally mesmerised, looking everywhere, in every possible location, tantalised, hypnotised and entranced by the smell. Although it spends its whole life searching it can never find it, because the poor deer doesn't realise that the smell is actually coming from its own navel and that the very thing it spends its whole life seeking is lying within itself.

Our human dilemma is just like this. Every day we set out to search for the source of the happiness which we know exists, but somehow just keep missing at every turn. Sometimes we may touch upon it briefly and think we have found the source, only to find it has disappeared again, forcing us to begin our search once more in another direction.

The reason why this kind of happiness is so tenuous is that circumstances can change very rapidly. If a place you love suffers an earthquake, it may be difficult for you to experience happiness there again. If someone who makes you very happy leaves, the happiness goes with them. If springtime is normally a very happy time for you and your loved one dies during the spring, it is possible that you will not be able to feel joyful the next time spring returns.

desires

The wanting mind is a symptom of our yearning for peace and happiness. Its nature is such that it spurs us endlessly on to acquire objects of desire such as delicious food or material possessions. It takes us to far-away places and leads us into wonderful relationships. It makes us do anything that we think will give us the feeling of fulfilment we yearn for.

**Of course, the truth is that no thing, time,
place or person can give us happiness.**

---

the ELUSIVE sweet CHILLI

There once was a young man who arrived home one day to find his father sitting at the kitchen table eating chillies, one after the other. Tears were streaming down his face, which was red and swollen.
'Are you enjoying those chillies, Dad?' he asked.
'No! They are awful,' replied the father.
'Then why keep eating them if they are making you feel so uncomfortable and unhappy?'
'Because,' he said, 'I am sure that soon I am going to find one that is sweet.'

The problem with desire is that it breeds more desires which can never, ever be satisfied. Desire can never end or reach a point of satisfaction, and yet somehow we always think that it will. This actually creates a deep sense of frustration within us because we know that the potential of happiness exists within each desire and yet somehow it eludes us every time, leaving us feeling empty and confused. This is what Mother Teresa calls 'spiritual deprivation'.

brief encounters

You can touch upon it briefly. When you see a beautiful sunset, for instance, in that moment there is peace within you, happiness wells up inside and everything feels right. The reason you feel so happy is simply because you have no inclination to change the situation or to make it other than it is in that moment.

total acceptance
In other words, you are in a situation of *total acceptance*. When you listen to a piece of music you love, you accept all the sounds unconditionally, becoming attuned to them for that span of time. While listening you feel whole and complete because there is no confusion or conflict within you.

So what is the happiness we are all searching for?

In essence, everyone is looking for a feeling of completeness or wholeness. People long to feel totally adequate and content with themselves as they are and with life as it is, instead of feeling fragmented and incomplete. The degree of adequacy you feel is very important in the understanding of the human condition, because it relates to how much you feel at home with yourself.

**A human being
who feels completely adequate
in any situation or circumstance
is one who comes close
to true and lasting happiness.**

So, if your degree of adequacy is dependent upon having champagne and caviar for breakfast, you might find yourself feeling very inadequate sharing dry bread and milk with a monk!

self-rejection
A feeling of inadequacy can lead you to reject yourself. This self-rejection only leads further into the cycle of desire-orientated pursuits, in the vain search for fulfilment. This, in turn, leads to more suffering.

self-acceptance
There is only one antidote to this problem and that is simply - self-acceptance. This is a major step towards true peace of mind - accepting yourself as you are now - unconditionally.

**The wanting mind
is a symptom of the mind's confusion
about what actually gives true happiness
and contentment in life.**

---

the WISH-FULFILLING tree

One day a man sat down under a huge tree to rest and shelter from the heat of the sun. Unbeknown to him, it was a wish-fulfilling tree. He lay down beneath it, gently daydreaming about the things he would like to have in his life.

He thought to himself, as people do, 'I would love to live in a beautiful palace with mother-of-pearl towers.' In a flash, the most exquisite palace appeared in front of him, its towers glistening in the afternoon sun. He stared in disbelief as it began to dawn upon him that his wish had actually become a reality. He tried it out again, 'I wish I could have some servants to work in the palace.' Sure enough a row of servants appeared before him. 'My goodness!' he thought, 'this is wonderful! I wish I could have an array of exotic foods.' A banquet appeared which he proceeded to devour with great relish and excitement as he pondered over the realisation that he could now have anything he wanted.

'I wish I could have a beautiful woman to share my palace with me.' In the winking of an eye she had appeared. They enjoyed each other's company for some time and then another thought came into his head. 'I wonder what would happen if this woman turned into a tiger.' Unfortunately, that too came to pass; in the next instant she had devoured him!

---

the way through

So, having recognised our dilemma, the question is, how are we going to get out of the cycle we have become so enmeshed in?

recognition

We have to recognise what is happening within us, and this usually results in such a deep feeling of pain or discontentment with life that it forces us to reach out for an alternative solution.

determination

From that point a feeling of *determination to change your life* begins to arise. It is essential to reach this point in order to be able to turn the tide towards freedom, because the restless mind does not want to change.

focus your mind

Now you need to begin to focus the mind from a point of calmness and this can only come about through silent sitting.

clarity

Sitting in silence brings about clarity in the mind. This is vital if you are to discern what your goal in life actually is. You can then take the necessary steps to bring yourself closer to freedom from suffering.

discrimination

From clarity, discrimination is born. Discrimination means being able to assess the appropriate response to life. It gives you a clear vision of your goal and brings about the wisdom to follow the correct path that will lead you to a calm, clear mind.

perseverance

From discrimination comes staying power or *perseverance*, which is essential if you are going to re-train the mind so that it can be used to help you. With training, the mind can become your greatest friend, instead of your greatest enemy. Staying power stems from a strong conviction of really knowing what it is that brings happiness that is lasting rather than temporary and fleeting.

Permanent happiness means being with yourself without conflict.

CONTENTMENT through helping OTHERS

In Uganda, FWF walked into a seminar hall to be greeted by forty pairs of tired eyes belonging to people who had committed their working lives to caring for those afflicted by AIDS.

Their job is to build not just a counselling relationship, but a one-to-one friendship with about forty five terminally ill people each week. In practice they have to work with nearly one hundred and fifty people every week with very little pay and, if they are lucky, only a bicycle to get them from one person to another.

We wondered what could possibly motivate people to give so much of themselves to others. Then we realised that probably everyone in that room had also been diagnosed HIV positive, without the full-blown symptoms of AIDS.

Knowing that their lives now had a time limit, these people were looking for contentment and success by sharing themselves and every single ounce of their strength with those around them.

AIDS counsellors in Uganda

It is not necessary to become terminally ill to realise what true contentment is. We each have the power to change our minds in every moment, to decide what we want to achieve in life and which direction we want to take.

17

Practical Peace Exercises *1*

♦ Sit quietly in a comfortable position and focus your mind
on a habit that you would like to change.
Breathe in to the count of six.
Breathe out to the count of four.
Practise for ten breaths.

♦ Now focus upon the quality you would like to replace it
with.
Breathe in to the count of four.
Breathe out to the count of six.
Practise for twenty breaths.
For maximum effect practise for thirty days. Try not to
miss a day.

♦ Think three times before you speak and ask yourself:
Is this true?
How will it affect others?
Is it really necessary?

♦ Take time out to go on a retreat to help you to gain a
perspective on where your life is going.

AT A GLANCE

THE SEARCH FOR HAPPINESS AND SUCCESS

1 Everyone is looking for happiness, peace and contentment and this search motivates every human endeavour.

2 Desire is a symptom of our longing for peace and the wanting mind drives us on an endless search for happiness - in people, places and material possessions.

3 Desire breeds more desire, never bringing satisfaction until we discover that happiness can only be found within ourselves.

4 Happiness comes when we feel:
- ◆ completely adequate
- ◆ at home in every situation in life
- ◆ total acceptance

5 Self-rejection is the result of feeling inadequate. Self-acceptance is the antidote!

6 How do we get out of this cycle?
- ◆ recognise what is happening
- ◆ decide to change
- ◆ focus the mind
  persevere!

'You are surrounded by treasure,
so there is no need to search.'

Tamo-san

THE NEED FOR A
CALM CLEAR MIND

calm, clear mind
silence
meditation
introspection

Calm Clear Mind

I f happiness and peace is our natural state, why aren't we aware of our peaceful nature?

It is because of the confused and restless mind, which for most of us is like a monkey that jumps endlessly from one thought to the next. These thoughts can take us from the heights of joy to the depths of despair.

to the calm mind all things are possible
Successful moments are those that are born from a point of calmness and I have found that decisions made in a calm state of mind are always the right ones.

what is a calm mind?
A calm mind is one which is never disturbed, no matter what happens. Having a calm mind allows us to accept and respond to what we experience in life, rather than reacting to it. This is not achieved by control alone.

This acceptance of life comes naturally from a quiet mind. It enables us to to dive deep within ourselves and see the interconnectedness of life as it really is.

This state has been experienced by teachers from all the great traditions. In history we see that behind the lives of some of the greatest teachers like Mahatma Gandhi and Vivekananda, lies a life of silent contemplation which arises from and gives rise to a calm mind.

You may be thinking that such a state is beyond your reach, but it is possible for all of us to discover this calmness and peace. We just need to know what to do to still the restless and confused mind that is continually jumping from one thought to the next.

there are many methods
One can develop a calm mind through sustained attention, coupled with the practice of introspection and constant reflection. These practices can help you to experience a new depth in your life.

sustained attention
When the mind, body and intellect are allowed a concentrated focus, peace is born. It is from here that you can find a place of complete calmness - a place where you can rest within yourself.

meditation
A period of regular meditation gives you the space to discover something permanent in your life. When you meditate regularly you begin to realise a purpose for your existence and the true meaning of peace.

**External wars are nothing
compared to the inner wars.**

At this moment in time there are more than forty civil wars happening around the world, but inside each person there are hundreds of wars going on. If you count the number of people on this planet, it adds up to an incredible number of wars!

keeping busy
I think perhaps people are afraid to look at the chaos that exists within them, which leads to a constant pursuit of external activity. People often feel they must keep busy because if they stay still long enough, they might have to acknowledge the conflict within.

Japanese language
The Japanese language is written in character form and the concept of 'busy' is expressed by a character which, directly translated from ancient text reads, 'to lose one's heart, or one's centre'.

**Meditation is one of the most active stages
in human evolution.**

Time spent meditating is easily justified because what we are actually trying to do is to challenge the busy, and often chaotic, areas of our lives. Meditation brings us into a state of balance that creates very positive changes within and consequently all around us.

**Meditation allows us
to embrace the philosophy
that 'when there is peace inside,
there is peace outside.'**

calmness

When you are born, your whole being is immersed in a deep sense of calmness. This is your natural state - the way you were meant to be - with nine-tenths of your energy focused on calmness and the other one-tenth directed towards activity.

I think we all agree that most people are not experiencing this state of calm and tranquillity. Somewhere along the line the natural formula has become turned around so that nine-tenths of our energy goes into activity and achievement and only one-tenth into maintaining a calm disposition - if that!

make peace a priority

As it takes an immense focus of energy to nurture and maintain a state of calmness, perhaps we first have to reach a point in our life where that becomes the priority.

letting go

This means letting go of expectation, frustration and anger. If your business partner doesn't turn up - so what? If you burn the dinner - it doesn't matter! Just let it go and don't lose your peace of mind - it's just not a good exchange rate. If you focus your entire energy on this tranquillity and inner calmness, then all actions, achievements and results will take care of themselves.

silent sitting

First practise the art of silent sitting, taking time to make an appointment with yourself and to connect with that deep inner silence.

breathing

Correct breathing is a good way of focusing and is one of the most valuable tools of meditation. Incorrect breathing can create stress and agitation within the body.

When the breath is still, the mind becomes still.

Practical Peace Exercises *2*

♦ Breathe in deeply.
Exhale in stages, as follows.
Begin to breathe out, pause and say the word 'peace' in your mind. Continue to exhale, pause and repeat the word 'peace' again in the same way. Repeat until the exhalation is complete.
Practise this as slowly as you can without becoming breathless. You will probably find yourself pausing four or five times per breath. With practice the number of stages will increase.

♦ Sit down comfortably, place your left hand on your abdomen and your right hand upon your chest.
Breathe in deeply and feel the expansion of the abdomen.
Draw the breath up into your chest and feel it expand.
As you breathe out relax your shoulders, abdomen and chest in that order.
Repeat five times.

♦ Breathe in and retain your breath momentarily whilst repeating the word peace, peace, peace...
Breathe out in a relaxed way.
Repeat five times.

SILENCE

**Silence is related to action,
as a seed is to a tree.
Once the tree has grown,
the seed is nowhere to be found.**

Have you ever really allowed yourself to become totally immersed in silence? In this world of traffic, planes, radios and heavy machinery it is becoming increasingly more difficult, but with creativity and determination it is still possible!

Silence is the most precious gift we have available to us. Although it can seem an 'empty' experience, it is, in fact, full of richness, for it is from silence that everything originates. Silence embraces love, patience and wisdom, bringing clarity and discrimination to the mind.

Let me invite you into the great temple of silence. Like a beautiful swan arising from the stillness of a deep lake, you will emerge from a place that knows no agitation. You will begin to feel that you do not want the world to be anything other than it is, accepting everything with no need to struggle or compete.

So why not experiment and allow yourself a small measure of silence every day, and during that time, reflect upon the deep treasures it contains. Beginning your day with silence nurtures a tremendous respect for the will of the universe, as it teaches you to move in harmony with life, flowing with it instead of struggling against it, trusting instead of living in fear of what is going to happen next.

Try not to talk too much during the day, because excessive talking drains your energy, whereas periods of silence help you to gather and store energy. Become aware of when you are talking too much, and gently remind yourself to stop and conserve energy, so that you do not become exhausted by the end of the day.

Mahatma Gandhi used to observe a day of silence every Monday. Years ago he wrote, 'I started my weekly observance of a silence day as a means of gaining time to look after my correspondence, but now those twenty four hours have become a vital need.'

GOLDEN Lake Village

Golden Lake Village was full of happy, contented and peace-loving people. There was a tremendous amount of care and love between them, although they never spoke to each other. They did not have the power of language and their only form of communication was silence.

One day some travellers came through the village using a spoken language. This intrigued the elders of the village so much that they prayed to be given a language so they could speak to each other. In a dream it was revealed to the chief elder that everyone should come to the side of the Golden Lake at midday and drink the water, for the gift of language to be granted. The next day, the whole village assembled around the lake and drank the water as instructed. Immediately the villagers began to make sounds which began as a murmur but soon turned into a loud din.

That night a fight broke out in the village as a result of an argument. It turned into a brawl, which led to a fire that destroyed half the village. The elders reassembled and discussed the destruction that had been created by the spoken word. They decided to pray again - for the gift of language to be taken away so that the power of silence could be restored. The village immediately became peaceful and loving once again.

You can only discover the power of silence by trying it. Experiment and see what happens!

Practical Peace Exercises *3*

♦ As soon as you are awake, sit up in bed and just capture the silence for one minute.
Notice the difference it makes to your day.

♦ Try to take time in your busy day to be silent. Begin with half an hour during the week and gradually increase the time.

♦ For one half day every month, preferably at or around full moon, maintain complete silence. This involves mental as well as verbal silence, which means no reading, writing, watching television or listening to the radio.

MEDITATION

When we take time to be still, something very beautiful begins to happen within us. As human beings, we are conditioned to flow out to other people and that is fine, but we also need to gather and conserve our energy and to withdraw into ourselves.

effortless being

Meditation doesn't have to mean hours of sitting in a difficult posture. It is really about connecting with yourself and gathering together all the different parts of yourself so that you do not rush into the day feeling fragmented.

harmony

Meditation is a tool - a way to explore the reality of life. When practised regularly it helps you to maintain a state of perfect balance, and creates a feeling of inner harmony. In the stillness that unfolds, many revelations will come and transformations will begin to take place. You will start to appreciate the silence and peacefulness of your own being.

deep relaxation

The deep state of relaxation induced by meditation has a profound influence upon the harmful effects of stress. It has been confirmed by modern medical research that it reduces anxiety and tension and brings about an improvement in general health and well-being.

practice

The fruits of meditation can only be achieved by practice - with an open heart and mind - so that it becomes a living experience. By establishing a regular practice you will find that your life gains a whole new dimension. If you make it a regular habit to sit at the same times each day, preferably in the early morning when you awaken and last thing at night before you go to bed, the benefits will become more apparent.

make an appointment with yourself

Practise in quiet, comfortable surroundings. Unplug the phone, decide not to answer any door bells and commit yourself to the period of time you have allocated for your meditation practice. Resolve that this is your time for yourself.

At first you may find it difficult to keep still for a long time, but don't worry about this. Just begin by sitting for five minutes, making sure you don't cause any strain to joints and muscles that are not used to it. Gradually you will be able to build up your sitting time to twenty minutes or more without moving. Remember that meditation is like riding on the crest of a wave that carries you all the way to the shore. It should be effortless. Too often we try too hard to make things happen and sometimes the harder we try, the less we achieve.

Try not to eat a heavy meal before meditation and wear loose, comfortable clothing made of natural fibres such as cotton or wool. It is also very helpful to have a meditation shawl which is not used for anything else to wrap around yourself.

sitting

So that you can gain the full benefit from your meditation practice, it is important to master the art of sitting correctly. You can sit cross-legged or on an upright chair with your hands resting gently in your lap.

If you sit on the floor, sitting on the edge of a cushion helps to tilt the lower back forward slightly and you can support your knees with another cushion if necessary. If you sit in a chair, try to support yourself rather than leaning back, because it is important to keep the spine straight.

posture

Posture has an enormous effect upon the way we think and feel, and if your back is not straight, it will be difficult to maintain a focus of thought and energy throughout your practice. Once you are happy with your sitting posture, begin to gently straighten your spine and relax the shoulders.

concentration

It is very important to remember that meditation is active and not passive. Concentration is a vital part of your practice and you will find that it is necessary to attain a degree of concentration in order to withdraw your awareness from the senses.

inner attitude

Try not to have any expectations, but sit quietly with an attitude that you will achieve the very best from your meditation time.

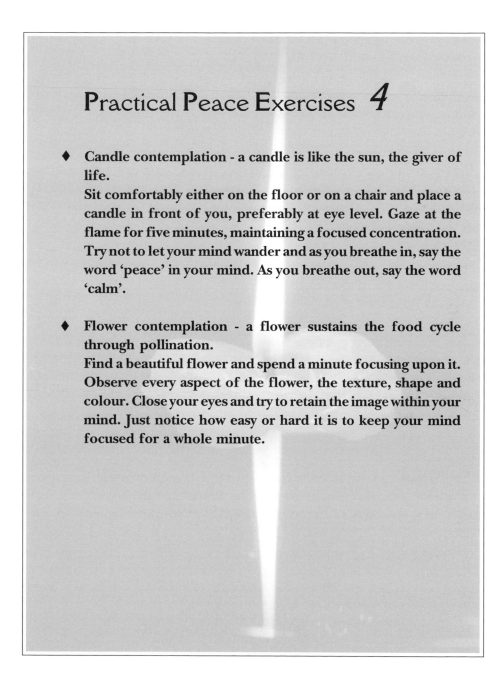

Practical Peace Exercises 4

♦ **Candle contemplation - a candle is like the sun, the giver of life.**
Sit comfortably either on the floor or on a chair and place a candle in front of you, preferably at eye level. Gaze at the flame for five minutes, maintaining a focused concentration. Try not to let your mind wander and as you breathe in, say the word 'peace' in your mind. As you breathe out, say the word 'calm'.

♦ **Flower contemplation - a flower sustains the food cycle through pollination.**
Find a beautiful flower and spend a minute focusing upon it. Observe every aspect of the flower, the texture, shape and colour. Close your eyes and try to retain the image within your mind. Just notice how easy or hard it is to keep your mind focused for a whole minute.

INTROSPECTION

Introspection is a very simple technique which, if you use it every day, will bring a sparkle of newness to your life, enabling you to live each moment as it arises.

Everyone is partly aware of the power of the subconscious mind, but perhaps we are not all aware of how we can actually gain access to that power.

Everything we receive through our five senses is channelled through the conscious mind and is stored subconsciously as deep feelings. Einstein used to say that a human being only uses about ten per cent of his inherent potential. The practice of introspection can help us to facilitate the flow of energy and power from the subconscious mind.

the technique of introspection
- Silent sitting and reflection
- Review
- Substitution
- Anchoring using the breath

silent sitting and reflection
Every evening, about half an hour before you go to sleep, gently and quietly reflect upon the day that has just been.

review
Do not criticise or judge any of your actions but simply go through each hour with awareness, and review each stage of the day.

substitution
When reviewing, every time you encounter a negative experience, replace the negative encounter with a positive image that is constructive - that is, how you would have liked it to be.

Think about how you would have preferred to see yourself acting and replace any impatience with patience, any anger with loving interactions and any resentment with forgiveness and acceptance.

For instance, if you have had trouble with your mother-in-law, imagine yourself giving her a bunch of flowers every time you see her. You will be amazed how your relationship with her will visibly improve!

anchoring
Concentrating on your breath during the process of substitution will empower your resolve to create a new, positive reality.

When you go to sleep after this process, the subconscious then dictates all these changes to the conscious mind and within a few days you will start interacting in a very positive and enriching way. You will find that events at work and at home which provoked anger in the past, will now be handled with gentle and peaceful understanding.

summary
- Sit quietly in a warm and relaxing environment.
- Quickly review the events of the day, hour by hour.
- Substitute all negative interactions with positive ones.
- Focus upon calm, deep breathing to empower the process.
- Each day, reflect and review the changes of the previous day.

Maintain this daily for a few weeks in order to see lasting changes. You will be surprised how easy it is to become a fully dynamic and joyful personality through this very simple and effective technique.

If you feel really enthusiastic and would like to add yet another dimension to this process, try keeping a journal to monitor the positive changes that are happening in your life. You will find it will become a great source of encouragement and inspiration to you.

AT A GLANCE

THE NEED FOR A CALM, CLEAR MIND

1   Happiness or peace is our natural state.

2   To the calm, clear mind all things are possible. A calm, clear mind is one that is never disturbed - no matter what happens. We do not know our peaceful nature because of the restless, monkey mind.

3   How can we cultivate a calm, clear mind?
It is not just a matter of controlling the mind, but of cultivating a balanced approach to life through:
- Silent sitting
- Meditation
- Introspection
- Breathing exercises

4   What are the most important qualities we need to make this work for us?
Determination to make peace a priority in our life.
Perseverance - and letting go of the inner wars:
- frustration
- anger
- expectation

'The hope of all men in the last analysis,
is simply for peace of mind.'

The Dalai Lama

'You have the potential to be like the great oceans,
like the trees and the mountains,
strong, determined - full of destiny and purpose.'

Mansukh

MY RELATIONSHIP WITH MYSELF

relating to yourself
loving yourself
inner ecology
believe in yourself
self esteem

RELATING TO YOURSELF

'Satyam eva jayate' - may truth rule victorious

Our whole life actually revolves around relationships, because whatever we do is determined by the way we relate to the people we live and work with. The way in which we perceive our relationships is also fundamental to the way we see ourselves and how we run our life.

Let's consider what it is that everyone looks for in relationships. We have already established that we all need to feel complete or whole and are searching for a feeling of oneness with something that we believe will free us from our pain, anguish, restlessness and even boredom.

So often we feel that we are lacking certain qualities which we would love to have. If we meet someone who seems to portray those qualities we can experience an overwhelming need to become attached to them. We feel happy to be around them because they add an extra dimension to our life, becoming a pillar to lean on in times of trouble.

But what if that person goes through a traumatic time in their life which changes them in some way? They can seem to lose the qualities that were once so admirable and unless the bond between you is very deep, the 'beloved one' can suddenly become a burden, no longer able to inspire or please in the same way.

Relationships of this kind are based on a personal and selfish need - which means that you want them because they make you happy or provide what you 'need', which is really an expression of one's own feeling of inner inadequacy.

However, through the depth of our experiences, we soon discover that we cannot always find completeness in relationships, places or things. We finally come to realise that totality and completeness are simply not inherent there.

Fear and doubt about this realisation can be erased by simply accepting that what you are seeking lies inside you and can only come from inside.

establish a relationship with yourself

Once you can accept this truth, it is then necessary to establish a relationship with yourself that fulfils all your needs. To fully appreciate the fact that you are already whole and complete, you will have to knock down the pillars of selfishness, hatred, greed and desire. Replace them with what you could call honest qualities such as truthfulness, selfless love, non-aggression and self-responsibility.

truth

Being truthful to yourself and others is fundamental to achieving peace in your life. People like Mahatma Gandhi and Martin Luther King based their lives on upholding truth and non-violence and just look at the incredible changes they were able to achieve for their countries.

four parts of yourself

Everyone is made up of the *knower*, the *thinker*, the *feeler* and the *doer*. If these are radically divided, as they are in any situation involving conflict and falsehood, then our whole personality becomes fragmented.

Whenever you deviate from truth, you will invite pain and suffering into your life because when you tell an untruth, it creates a split within your personality.

For instance, if a man buys a car for £400 and the next day his friend offers to buy it for £500, he stands to make an honest profit. But what if he tells him he paid six hundred pounds for it? On the one hand he has goodness urging him to tell the truth, and on the other greed is telling him to lie. If the man rejects truth for the sake of acquiring money, he opens the door for unhappiness to enter. His personality becomes divided, and this will radically affect all other aspects of his life. You know that feeling when you wake up in the morning - when you, the 'knower', want to get up early but you, the 'doer', will switch off the alarm clock, throw it across the room and go back to sleep?

be honest with yourself

Being truthful to yourself leads to having conviction in your life. It integrates and unifies your whole personality, which means you are able to uphold your convictions in life.

self-responsibility

The energy that comes from your conviction supports you and everything you set out to do, bringing fulfilment in your own self-responsibility.

My workshops on stress management with psychiatrists reveal that many of their patients show a positive recovery when offered the opportunity to take responsibility for their lives. In my experience, wherever people are self-responsible they are happy, prosperous and excited about life as well as light-hearted, full of humour, laughter and clear insight.

Those who deny responsibility and all involvement with their environment, sit in the comfort of their own cage, thinking and believing that there is no-one else out there. We are all part of the web of life and we have a responsibility towards ourselves and each other.

LOVING YOURSELF

Life is all about exploration and investigation, in an attempt to comprehend its meaning and understand the way we relate to ourselves, each other and the whole of the universe.

The journey, of course, can only start with each one of us individually. It is only when we have developed a perfect relationship with ourselves that we can ever hope to achieve a perfect relationship with anyone else – the people around us and the greater whole.

**How do I discover the strength to make my life
a dramatic, fulfilling adventure?
By building a strong relationship with myself.**

love yourself
Self-love means relating to yourself with love and affection instead of condemnation and criticism. Accepting yourself as you are gives you a platform from which you can begin to make real and lasting changes. Self-condemnation only empowers imperfections and does not assist the process of self-transformation.

the innner smile
The secret is to develop the 'inner smile', which is an attitude that supports and enhances the sunny side of yourself. I heard a lovely story recently about a little boy who was putting his shoes on one day when his mother said to him, 'Your shoes are on the wrong feet, Jim!' The little boy looked at his feet, then at his mother in total amazement and said, 'But Mum! These are the only feet I've got!'

Look for the humour in every situation and learn to laugh at yourself.

honour your body
We have all been blessed with some very simple gifts which perhaps we take for granted and do not respect as much as we could. For instance, think about your body. It is so important that your relationship with your body is a harmonious one.

If you despise your body, you will actually invite sickness and disease which destroys the beautiful gift that the universe has given you. If you can recognise and really honour the gifts that your body, mind and senses bring, you will then be able to really love who you are unconditionally. Learn to understand that your body, mind and spirit will lead you into greater reverence for yourself. When you unite all the different parts of yourself, wholeness is born.

honouring through appreciation

So, recognising this need, how do you then develop a feeling of reverence for your body? In this chapter we will explore how to develop a sense of humour and respect for all the different parts of yourself, taking time to admire and appreciate the miracle of the body's functions.

your eyes

With your eyes you can witness eternity in the stars. You can see mountains wrapped in veils of mist, or enveloped by the golden curtain of the setting sun. You can watch the moonlight glistening over the sea at night, or leaves swirling and dancing in the wind.

your ears

With your ears you can hear beautiful sounds like the melody of the wind, the roar of the ocean, the song of a river. Can you imagine not being able to hear the bubbling laughter of a child or the first sounds of the dawn chorus? Listening with care to the music of nature can bring such a beautiful sense of the continuity of life and unity with all living things.

your voice

Your voice enables you to communicate with love and concern. It allows you to sing and express the beauty and joy within.

Once you have begun to appreciate the myriad and wonderful functions of the body you live in, you then need to keep the body and mind as clear as possible.

good diet

Eat well, because a wholesome diet and appreciation for food brings inner strength to the body and mind, and this strength enables you to endure circumstances that may be very trying. It is through endurance and tolerance that you gain a deeper insight into the secret of enjoying each living moment. Having this insight frees you from being caught up in, and overwhelmed by the challenges that present themselves to you every day of your life.

Make your meals a peaceful, relaxed experience, filled with care and respect for the food and its preparation. You will find that you will actually 'eat' these positive qualities and your day will be far more harmonious. Likewise, food that is produced and prepared in a kind and loving environment will taste better and be more satisfying. The reason Mum's food always tastes best is because of the love she puts into it.

The vegetarian approach is less harmful to the earth and a more compassionate way to eat. According to the Vegetarian Society, one person will eat 1,000 animals in their lifetime. Every minute of every working day, 5,787 animals die in this country alone. Statistics show that over 5,000 people a week change to a vegetarian diet and 13,000 each week are cutting red meat out of their diet. This indicates that more and more people are adopting a compassionate approach to eating. Probably most of your diet is vegetarian already, but if not, it might be nice to consider eating less meat. Perhaps you could eat meat every other day instead of every day. Please consider this because it can greatly help towards the restoration of the earth.

breathing
Breathing correctly is a simple and wonderful way to bring about a sense of well-being and clear-thinking. When you breathe fully and freely, you are drawing life energy into the body, refreshing and enlivening every cell. This has a cleansing effect upon your whole body and mind. Calm, conscious breathing brings steady discrimination, enabling you to avoid being swallowed up by the desires of life. Breathing in this way can help you to perceive everything from a different perspective, so that challenges become opportunities.

exercise
In order to create physiological balance the body needs to be exercised.

As it expands and contracts with movement, the process of detoxification is also stimulated.

develop mental ecology

Try to read things that inspire and uplift your spirit. Words written by those who understand life from a greater depth and intensity will help you to gain clarity and perspective and to understand the importance of keeping your thoughts positive and uplifting.

listening

Take time to listen to people who have a positive influence upon you and who are doing things that bring harmony into their own lives. Try not to spend time with people who are not reaching out to life in a positive way, for if you mix with thieves you will eventually become one, and if you mix with angels, that's what you will become!

use the senses selectively

Do you remember as a child feeling that each moment was so exciting, that there was a tremendous thrill about everything and a certainty that something very beautiful was about to unfold in each moment?

I truly believe that it is possible to revive this way of thinking, feeling and being, so that every new moment can once again be anticipated with excitement. You can look forward to it with a sense of suspense whilst at the same time feeling detached and calm, knowing that anything may happen. By choosing to be selective in your use of the senses, you will find that you are suddenly presented with a whole variety of new ways to interact with them.

I will not attempt to uncover all the different variations here, all the beauty and manifestations, as this can become a very joyful and exciting personal discovery. In any one moment you can become exposed to something you have never touched, tasted or felt before - something that can become a very beautiful catalyst for making your relationship with yourself a more harmonious and evolving one.

Practical Peace Exercises 5

♦ Sit quietly and begin to focus on your breathing. Breathe in, to the sound SO - the sound that the inbreath naturally makes. Breathe out to the sound HAM. Meditate upon these sounds for five minutes as you gently breathe in and out.

As you expand your awareness into the SO HAM breath, it will bring your senses into focus and heighten your awareness of yourself.

♦ Try not to expose yourself to the media. Bad news has a tendency to cultivate a negative attitude to life.

♦ Make your health a priority. A regular exercise programme like swimming or jogging will assist you in maintaining a positive self-image.

♦ Eat plenty of fresh vegetables and fruit. Try to be aware of how much your diet affects your well-being.

♦ Finish your day with these high thoughts:

'Everything about me is perfect and wonderful.'
'I honour and respect everything that I am.'

INNER ECOLOGY

The **Peace Formula** is all about inner ecology, which means creating a peaceful environment that starts from inside yourself and therefore uplifts the world around you rather than polluting it.

Brazilian environmentalists

There is an umbrella group of environmental organisations in Rio de Janeiro called Apadema, which is at the forefront of a new movement which is sweeping the environmental world. It works on the idea of *inner ecology*, which is based on the fact that if there is corruption within ourselves or in the workplace, then the environment will inevitably suffer.

the power of negative thoughts

It is becoming increasingly obvious that if individuals, whether they are top politicians or just ordinary people in society, are thinking negative thoughts, then sooner or later those thoughts are going to be reflected in their actions. Each word we speak and every thought we think creates an energetic ripple effect that radiates out into the world influencing everything and everyone around us.

Imagine the domino effect on the world when you have a whole society expressing negative thoughts.

mind pollution

If we are not careful, we can actually pollute the atmosphere around us with the thoughts we are thinking and our consequent actions. This means that we all have a tremendous responsiblity to choose our words with care and to temper negative thoughts if we really want to contribute towards a better world.

become the creator of your own destiny

Every human being in every country and culture has been given a tremendous treasure - the secret of the whole universe within their own being. This secret contains the very power, nature and function of everything that exists. Knowing this enables us to become the creator instead of the victim of our life.

**You are the creator
of your own destiny
because the universe just
responds to your command.**

In fact our thoughts play a much more important role than most people realise. We have such a great responsibility because our thoughts actually create the universe around us. How is this possible?
My father used to say that if you want to understand the universal force, it is represented by one echo, which is YES, YES, YES.

Have you ever bought a car and thought to yourself, 'I don't want my new car to get a scratch,' and within two days it's scratched? If you work with the negative thought form, it will happen! You might have to think about this for a while! Whatever you say, the universe says 'yes' to it. If you are thinking negatively, those thoughts are empowered by that force, and of course the same applies to your positive, enlivening thoughts.

**The universe is not bad,
the world is not bad,
life is not bad -
it does not do anything to you.**

flow with life

Newton's Law of Motion states: 'To every action, there is an equal and opposite reaction'. So if you take off your shirt and rub your back against a tree, you will get a reaction in terms of a very sore back, but the tree didn't do anything to you. Likewise, if you rub against life, going against the flow of the universe, life will become very uncomfortable.

---

the POWER of PRAYER

Two men were being chased by a tiger. One man shouted to the other, 'Quick, say a prayer or we will be done for! I don't know any!'
The other man shouted back, 'I only know the one my father used to say!'

'That'll do - anything! Anything!'

The man began, 'For what we are about to receive, may the Lord make us truly grateful!'

By our own choice, by the very nature of our thoughts and attitudes, we have attracted to us many things that have happened in our life.

like attracts like

If you are full of excitement and adventure, then you will become surrounded by similar people simply because like attracts like.

I know of a lady in Hong Kong who has survived cancer by building a positive attitude to life. Like most people in Hong Kong she lived in a skyscraper, which can be thirty to forty floors high. She once told me about one particular evening when she had arrived home late, about midnight, to discover that she had left her key inside her apartment. Her husband and son were also both out.

She said to herself, 'At this point I can either get frustrated about what is happening, or I can sit here and enjoy this opportunity to be with myself.' She waited and waited and two hours later her son appeared in the lift. She greeted him ecstatically, much to his surprise, and then he realised what had happened. His face fell when he further realised that he had also forgotten his key! They had no idea how long it would be before her husband came back and for the next fifteen minutes they waited in agony.

She said that those fifteen minutes were a much greater trial than the whole two hours she had previously spent waiting.

develop a positive attitude

Her first two hours demonstrate how cultivating a good attitude can affect your life's experiences. Her final, long drawn-out fifteen minutes illustrate the need to work continually at cultivating a positive attitude in life.

Your life is an incredible gift.
It is not a struggle, but a challenge to meet.
It is a tool for growth and for experience.

When we come to recognise the incredible power that lies within us, and the potential that is there, we must not misuse it. Having discovered such a beautiful secret, we must begin to empower the goodness and gentleness of life with our thoughts. Then we can start to help others who are in need, becoming more selfless in our actions and activities and less self-concerned.

Let us use this power to uphold and protect life
rather than destroy and uproot it.

Practical Peace Exercises *6*

♦ **Standing Meditation**
This is a wonderful centering technique to help to align and balance all the energy centres in the body.

Stand straight and tall, feet together, shoulders open and arms relaxed by your sides.
Allow yourself to rock gently on your feet from side to side.
Imagine you are like a grandfather clock with a pendulum swinging inside you.
See the pendulum swinging gently within you and allow it to gradually slow down.
Now stop! As if someone has just snapped their fingers.
See the pendulum hanging straight and still within you.
Now rock gently backward and forward and repeat the process in the same way.
You will feel calm, centred and balanced - ready to face anything!

♦ Set aside one hour a day to dedicate to your personal inner ecology. Be aware of your thoughts within that time, especially noting your responses and interactions with others. Once this has been successfully explored, lengthen the time to a morning, then a whole day.

BELIEVE IN YOURSELF

I magine a human being who enters each moment without any hesitation, fear or shyness, but instead settles into the moment with kindness and joy, exploring it and expanding with it. Visualise a human being who is full of happiness, always laughing and smiling, full of enthusiasm and aspiration.

This person is expressing a total belief in himself.

Every human being is endowed with such a tremendous power, ability and strength.

the power of choice

Everyone has been given the free will to choose in each moment whether to be happy or sad, clear or confused, full of inspiration or depressed. We always have the choice either to despise and wound others, or to be kind and respectful to them.

We have the ability to choose to believe in hope and faith as opposed to hopelessness and doubt. We have the choice to look at every challenge in life as a gift through which we can transform ourselves and become better, stronger and more peaceful human beings.

This simple privilege does not involve anyone else, for there is no striving for wealth or fame involved, or even dreams for the future. The only person involved is you, in this moment, now.

self-condemnation

You need to give yourself permission to be what you want to be and the first and most important thing to do is to stop condemning yourself. There is no greater danger for a human being than self-condemnation, because it takes away the very essence of power that can make everything happen for you. It takes away inspiration and all possibility of ever succeeding.

So from this moment on please don't waste any time in condemning the spirit that you are. From this moment on, erase from your vocabulary words like 'can't' and 'impossible'. Everything in life is possible. The only limitations you have are those you impose upon yourself. Take away the limitations born of ignorance and untruth and you will never experience another moment of sorrow.

remove all limitations

Replace 'I cannot' with 'I can' and miracles will begin to happen. Every time you find yourself saying 'I cannot swim', or 'I cannot sing', or 'I cannot be strong and positive', change it around and begin to empower the truth about yourself. I always try to start every day with self-inspiration and never limit myself. When you do this your life starts to change and even the people around you will change.

believe in yourself - believe in what you are

Believe in the words you speak, the actions you carry out and every feeling that comes into your heart. Believe in yourself with all your heart,

Orphan from Croatia - Eurowalk 2000

mind and spirit. Be kind to yourself, and then you will be full of strength and an inspiration to others. Be full of faith in yourself, and then just watch what happens.

**'As human beings, our greatness lies
not so much in being able to remake the world,
as in being able to remake ourselves.'**

Mahatma Gandhi

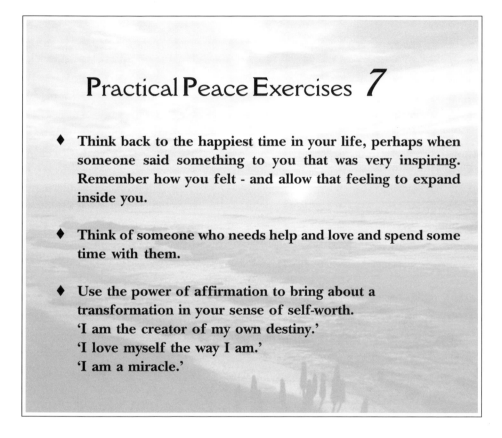

Practical Peace Exercises *7*

♦ **Think back to the happiest time in your life, perhaps when someone said something to you that was very inspiring. Remember how you felt - and allow that feeling to expand inside you.**

♦ **Think of someone who needs help and love and spend some time with them.**

♦ **Use the power of affirmation to bring about a transformation in your sense of self-worth.
'I am the creator of my own destiny.'
'I love myself the way I am.'
'I am a miracle.'**

SELF-ESTEEM

L et us now explore the importance of self-esteem. I think it is fair to say that for most of our lives we judge our state of well-being on the basis of how we are feeling within ourselves and how worthy we feel in any situation. I have talked about this at length in the first chapter, so you might say that that this is not a new concept - and it isn't - but just stay with me a little bit longer.

Most of our lives are spent within a syndrome of approval and disapproval from others.

What does that mean? In simple terms, it means that if someone comes up to you and says, 'You are wonderful!' you feel happy and a lovely feeling wells up inside. If on the same day, someone says to you, 'I really don't think you are very nice,' it can affect you so dramatically as to turn your whole day from one of happiness and positivity to one of total negativity.

So what you are doing is giving your power away to other people.

Is our happiness so fragile and so much determined by the way others see us? If we can really understand how we are relating to others it can make a lot of difference to how we balance ourselves and make the best of our inner potential.

understand the nature of power
The word 'power' contains a sense of dynamism, control and freedom. When life is based upon constant approval from others, the way our day unfolds will depend upon how much power we give to other people.

Being constantly dependent upon other people's approval creates a great leakage of energy from within us. We give power to other people when we feel we want them to love or like us and therefore the nature of power and the nature of love are closely interlinked.

empower yourself

How then do you give love to people without giving your power away to them? How can you learn to feel so powerful internally that you no longer depend on approval from others?

There is only one way. You have to empower what you have already got. You have to pull in the antennae that are out searching for approval and charge yourself up internally.

---

the NURSE with the KIND VOICE

I once knew a nurse, a very beautiful woman whom everybody loved. One day she was hurt in a serious accident and her face became so disfigured that people could hardly bear to look at her.

As a result she was forced to give up the job she loved, because it involved being in the public eye all the time. The poor woman was plunged into the depths of despair, not knowing what to do, because her one love in life was nursing. She became chronically depressed. One day a friend took her to visit a home for blind children, where she met and played with the children. As she became aware of these beautiful children, she began to forget about her own problems. They could not see her face and so they were relating to her on a different level.

One child said to her, 'You must have the prettiest face in the world, because your voice is so kind.'

This lady consequently was offered a job in the children's home and began to realise that her real value as a human being did not depend on her appearance but on something much, much deeper within her.

This story shows us that we have to look deeper into ourselves and our lives. The nurse's real beauty was on the inside, in her care and love for people.

accept yourself

So make the best of what you have. We are all unique. To be able to accept yourself as you are is a wonderful step towards self-esteem. If you start accepting yourself, you begin to believe in yourself. If you don't believe in yourself, nobody else will.

thoughts are magnetic

If you have a poor image of yourself, with low self-esteem and self-worth, that is the image others will have of you. What you think - you attract. This is the simple law of the universe. If you think you are nothing, that's what you will be. Believing in yourself is the first step towards others believing in you because the nature of thought is attraction.

If you think you are the best dancer, that is what you will become. Why? Because the energy that exudes from you is the message that everyone picks up. A confident person is one who has faith in himself and that confidence is then confirmed by other people.

Self-acceptance is crucial if you are to make any headway towards self-esteem. Accept yourself as you are. Accept the beauty that you are; look for it and then understand that everything is beautiful.

real beauty is on the inside

The concept of beauty varies from one person to another. If a 'beautiful' person says something unkind, your whole impression of that person will change. But someone who is not so physically attractive can appear beautiful because of their kindness and joy.

you become what you believe

It is wise to base your life upon the firm ground of acceptance instead of non-acceptance. If you can accept yourself as you are and start to feel your own worthiness, you will begin to radiate that energy naturally and it will return to you confirmed. Your natural wisdom will then empower others in the same way.

Take a look at how you interact with life and what sort of power relationships you create - don't give your power to other people. Contain your own power within yourself - the power that is to be found in silent sitting.

self-ESTEEM

When Noah was getting the animals onto his ark, an ant turned to the elephant next to him and said, 'Stop pushing - or else!'

Practical Peace Exercises *8*

◆ Make the first thought of your day an affirmation of something you would like to achieve in that day. Affirm this before you get up and before you say anything. If possible, write it down before you get up.

◆ This peace exercise will empower your whole day. It will bring you into an awareness of your personal power and help you to develop a sense of confidence in yourself.

'While one person hesitates because he feels inferior,
the other is busy making mistakes
and becoming superior.'

Henry C Link

AT A GLANCE

MY RELATIONSHIP WITH MYSELF

1   Develop the Inner Smile....

2   Accepting yourself as you are gives you a platform from which you can make real and lasting changes.

3   Discover how amazing you are by taking time to appreciate your body, mind and senses. Strengthen your body and clarify your mind through:
   - healthy diet
   - correct breathing
   - exercise
   - mental ecology

4   Give yourself a boost by choosing to be around positive and uplifting people, films and books.

5   Believe in yourself and choose:
   - to be happy, not sad
   - to have hope and faith
   - to stop condemning yourself
   - to remove all limitations
   - replace 'I cannot' with 'I can', 'I am not' with 'I am'

6   Realise the power of your own thoughts and that you can pollute the atmosphere with negative thoughts. The universe is totally positive and always says YES!

7   Live in Truth - you are the knower, thinker, feeler and doer. Any untruth in your life will cause conflict and weakness between these four parts of yourself.

8   Don't give your power away to others.

Friends from Japan at the Life International Conference

'Leaving the mind, enter the chambers of the heart -
where frontiers end and friendship begins.'

Mansukh

My Relationship with Others

right-understanding
living beyond conflict
the power of words
non-violence & fearlessness

Right Understanding

Life creates a beautiful backdrop upon which to see the negative qualities within yourself and the points you need to work on. Because the universe is constantly trying to help you to come nearer to your true self, it is very important to look at each event in your life as it arises, with right-understanding and right-perspective. Right-understanding helps you to look at your negative qualities in a positive way, with gentleness and willingness, and to appreciate and remove the ignorance which prevents you from seeing situations as they really are.

awareness

Every situation that presents itself comes to you so that you can learn from it and grow a little more in the awareness of what you truly are. How you look at a situation determines the results as it is neither good nor bad in itself.

tolerance

If you find your environment is distracting or agitating, try to see it as a reflection of what it is you need to work on. In any situation that is creating agitation, a lot of sensitivity is required - regardless of the knowledge you may possess. You will need to have calmness, patience, generosity and understanding.

Don't judge a man until you have walked a mile in his shoes.

right perspective

Put yourself in other people's shoes and try to understand where they are coming from and why. There are so many misconceptions and expectations as to how things should be in any one particular time and place. Try to appreciate that the universe is always trying to show you - in a very subtle way - exactly where you stand in any situation and often in places you have not even thought of before.

see things positively

The laughter and chuckle of a child, the glimpse of a beautiful ray of light, the stillness of a lake, or the beauty of creation all affect the heart centre and open channels of energy within us.

When you become caught by negativity, some of these energy channels will immediately become blocked and if you look at a situation from a negative viewpoint, that is exactly how it will present itself.

fear
Fear of the known and unknown presents a major obstacle to appreciating the true reality of things. There may have been situations in your childhood that created a fearful response within you, so that when something happens that reminds you of it, you will find yourself automatically reacting with that same fear.

accepting the past
You may feel that people in the past have hurt or wounded you in ways that are detrimental to your present life. Holding on to resentment and blame only hurts you, and does not create any changes within you. Change itself is instigated by the Law of Acceptance.

Nothing is a random event. When you realise that everything that has happened to you in your life was for a very good reason, you will find you can accept the past.

forgiveness
By accepting the past you are letting go of the idea of being a victim and taking responsibility for being the *creator* of your own life. This also means letting go of blame and criticism of others. Acceptance means forgiving others for their negativity and forgiving means that you begin to realise that others only did what they did because they thought it was right for you or themselves at the time.

Acceptance in your heart of others' wrongs and mistakes is a way of being sincere and truthful about how much your connection to others means to you.

appreciate people
None of us actually realise how much we are hurting others through our thoughts, words, actions and feelings. It may take months or even years to discover that something we said without thinking a long time ago has hurt a dear friend. It requires time, effort and commitment on our part to keep contact with those we love and care for.

affirmation

As we start to accept and understand through forgiveness, we will begin to develop a gentle calmness and a peaceful mind. Affirmations implant new and enlivening thought patterns into the mind and these powerful thoughts can assist the process of self-transformation, as forgiveness and acceptance begin to replace blame and resentment. We can never be truly at peace if we are holding on to painful memories.

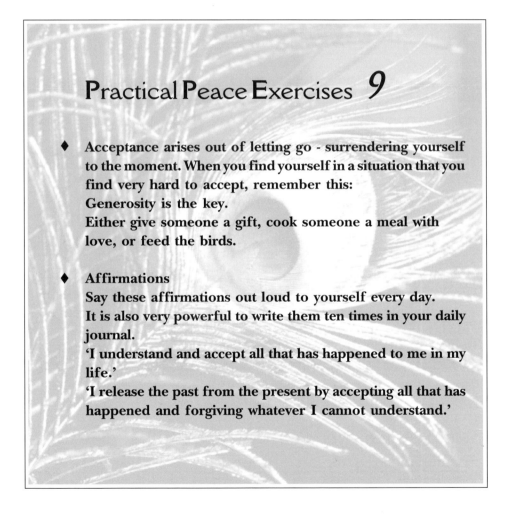

Practical Peace Exercises 9

♦ Acceptance arises out of letting go - surrendering yourself to the moment. When you find yourself in a situation that you find very hard to accept, remember this:
Generosity is the key.
Either give someone a gift, cook someone a meal with love, or feed the birds.

♦ Affirmations
Say these affirmations out loud to yourself every day.
It is also very powerful to write them ten times in your daily journal.
'I understand and accept all that has happened to me in my life.'
'I release the past from the present by accepting all that has happened and forgiving whatever I cannot understand.'

LIVING BEYOND CONFLICT

We have asked groups all over the world what they felt their goal was in terms of relating to others. Here are the most often voiced aspirations:

- to make friends easily
- to respond to people with laughter and enjoyment
- not to react critically or with judgement
- to relate with confidence to people
- to be able to stand firm with dignity when truth demands it
- to establish a relationship that is meaningful to both parties
- to be able to inspire and uplift
- to be able to trust people without fear
- to be able to interact peacefully and harmoniously

Everyone wants to be like this, but how do you do it?

One day recently, I was sitting under a tree on the children's swing. The sun was shining, the birds were singing and the mountains rose up majestically all around me. As I sat there, I was reminded of the first swing I had ever sat on in Kenya where I grew up. It all came back to me - the smell of the flowers that grew around my own little swing and even the feeling of the warm air that I used to feel upon my body. I remembered that my mother used to tell me many wonderful stories, even though she could neither read nor write. I began to wonder what it was that made my relationship with her so very special, that makes her memory so dear to me to this day. I realised that we were simply not afraid of each other.

I looked at the swing, the clouds, the mountains and the birds flying around me - but this immense beauty could not touch the memory of being with my mother in those precious moments. Being with her with no trace of fear between us had implanted something within me that gave me so much strength for the future.

letting go of fear
I feel that the first step towards resolving conflict in your life has to begin

with erasing fear in communication. This means that you have to start trusting people, and you can only do this if you resolve to see the very best in them.

never criticise
Begin by never criticising or condemning others. Let them be who they are, allowing them the freedom to express themselves in whatever way they feel is appropriate for them. Respond to people with laughter and enjoyment, in a constructive way rather than reacting critically.

accept others
Accepting others as they are brings a wonderful freedom to your own mind. You will begin to see that people's idiosyncrasies are actually quite endearing and you can start to really love them for who they are, however strange they may appear to be!

never judge
If we judge others, drawing harsh conclusions about them without even giving them a chance, we will never see the potential and the beauty that exists in every person. Spending your whole day in judgement and assessment of everything can only leave you drained and exhausted.

focus on love
In the face of conflict, it is important to give people freedom. Respond to each situation with respect and have more concern for the people involved than for the situation itself. Try not to concentrate on the problem, but look at the person or people. You can dislike the sin, but do not hate the sinner. If you focus on love, that is what will grow. Focus on hate and conflict and that will become the dominant factor, because what you focus on expands.

bless and appreciate others
So rather than condemning people, bless and appreciate them, focusing on their best qualities and empowering them to be the best they can be. This will bring you back into the oneness of life - and unity.

empower others
Be brave enough to tell people they are strong and not weak, because people's problems arise out of feeling weak, making them seek power

and strength in order to feel secure. When you feel weak, you want power over people - to rule over them - but if you are already strong, you do not need to have power over others.

If you are not seeking power over others, you will feel no need to impose upon anyone and instead simply appreciate and love them. No matter who it is, you have to give people a chance to be themselves. You will need to be accepting and a little bit forgiving so that you can feel comfortable with them. Once you begin to accept yourself, then you can move on to accept others as they are - unconditionally. Don't take away from people - give to them, for what you give comes back to you ten thousandfold.

try not to have expectations
Don't expect too much of others. For if you do, you may feel betrayed if they do not live up to your expectations. If you don't there is no chance of feeling let down, and in fact there is plenty of room to be pleasantly surprised.

forgiveness
If you want to make your relationship with others work, put forgiveness in the place of condemnation, expectation, criticism and judgement.

try not to be perfect
What is it that threatens people? If you spend all your time trying to create a perfect personality you can actually frighten people away - because you can become a threat to them. As a reflection for your consideration, don't try to appear perfect, but just be yourself.

---

the PERFECT man

A man once went to his doctor for help. 'Doctor, please help me. I am so depressed although I have no reason to be. I don't drink, · smoke or gamble. I am vegetarian, never hurt animals or people and go to church every Sunday. I have a perfect marriage and am popular and hard working. What am I doing wrong?'
'Aha!' said the doctor knowingly. 'I know what your problem is - your halo is too tight!'

It takes a lot of pressure off us when we let go of this need to be the best and the most perfect human being. It actually makes energy available to us that we can use for true centering.

to every action there is a reaction

When interacting with people, if you can remember to do as you would be done by, you will find your relationships will always be successful. Ask yourself how you would like others to treat you. How would you like to be spoken to? What would you like to happen to you? If you like to receive flowers or cards - then give someone flowers or send a lovely card. If you don't like to be spoken to harshly, then speak gently to others.

The Aboriginal people in Australia make decisions looking forward ten generations and back ten generations. If the decision to be made affects things in either direction, it has to be reconsidered. Perhaps we do not have to consider ten generations, but even thinking about how our actions affect others is a significant step forward. If more people could think twice before acting and speaking, so many unpleasant circumstances could be avoided.

If you find yourself at the end of the day feeling tired and unusually tight inside, be aware that this could be due to the fact that you may not have resolved interactions within your day which could have caused conflict within you.

There are many ways to resolve these feelings. Next time you find yourself feeling any kind of conflict - anger, hatred, rejection or pain - please sit down and place your right hand on your heart centre and your left hand on the area of your navel.

Simply allow a feeling of energy or warmth to flow between your hands from one point to the other, balancing and calming the emotions.

Now think about what it is that has upset you and identify the point of tension in your body. That is the place where you are holding the conflict. Place your right hand on that area. Hold it there for a few seconds. Try to go into the feeling and see the other side of it.

- If you feel sadness, look for joy.
- If you feel anger, look for forgiveness and understanding.
- If you feel impatience, look for patience and tolerance.

Allow the tension to gently soften under your hand. As it begins to melt, feel the calmness and the peace that remains. Smile!

Practical Peace Exercises *10*

♦ **The Crocodile Position**
Lie down on the floor on your front. Place your arms above your head and take hold of each elbow, resting your forehead on the forearms. Separate your legs as far apart as is comfortable and allow your heels to roll inwards. As you breathe, focus upon the movement of your abdomen against the floor.
This position stretches and releases the base of the spine and is extremely relaxing.

♦ **The Peace Position**
From an upright position allow your body to gently bend forward from the hips - just as far as you can comfortably go. Let your arms and head hang loosely. Breathe in, visualising a rising of awareness through your legs up to the heart and breathing out through your arms into the earth.
This is a great one to do in the garden! Stay for as long as you can, or until you feel a slight tingling in your calves and feet as unwanted energy blocks are released!

♦ **Visualisation**
Visualise someone you love very much and allow yourself to feel that love. Now superimpose the face of a person you are in conflict with upon that of your loved one. Allow the feeling of love to extend to them.
Affirm: 'I choose to forgive and let go and to create peace between us.'

THE POWER OF WORDS

If you want to resolve conflicts in your life and to avoid hurting people, it is really important to watch the way you use words.

words can wound

I once knew a thirty year old woman who was anorexic and weighed only four stone. Someone had once said to her, 'You are a fat and powerful woman.' That was it, she stopped eating and it destroyed her whole life, because those words had cut so deeply into her heart.

WORDS can HEAL

There once was a saint who was giving a discourse to a huge crowd of people in India. After he had finished talking, a young mother brought her baby to him to ask for healing as the child was seriously ill. He simply spoke a few words of blessing over the child.

A man suddenly stood up in the crowd and shouted, 'You can't just do that. How can a few words make any difference to this sick child?' The teacher looked at him and then proceeded to hurl abuse and insults at him. The man reacted by flying into a rage and ran towards the teacher with the intention of hitting him. Just before he got to him, the teacher raised his hand and said, 'Stop! Do you not see how my words have had the power to make you so angry? Why then should they not also have the power to heal? Words can heal or harm and that is why we should speak few words and when we do speak, we should make them kind and uplifting. If you cut others with your words, you cut yourself, and where is the wisdom in that?'

The man understood and fell at his feet in reverence.

I was very touched by the words of the wonderful Peace Pilgrim when she said, 'If I offend people I look at myself, for I know that if my conduct were correct, they would not have been offended. Before the tongue can speak it must have lost the power to wound.'

**Just as a skylark touches our hearts
with the sweetness of its song, let our words be pure and kind.
Let them soothe and heal, but never harm.**

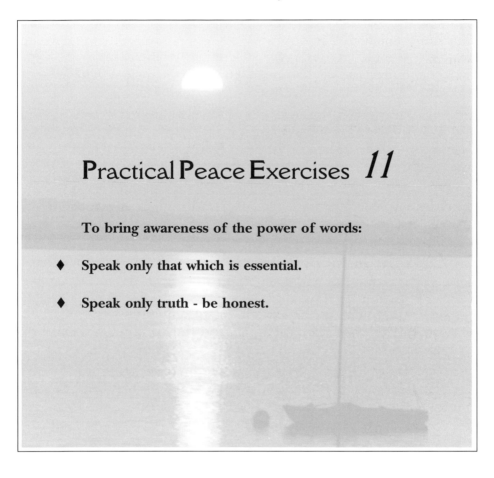

Practical Peace Exercises *11*

To bring awareness of the power of words:

♦   **Speak only that which is essential.**

♦   **Speak only truth - be honest.**

**'I discovered the secret of the sea,
in meditation upon the dewdrop.'**
Kahlil Gibran

Non-Violence and Fearlessness

Whilst in India, I met a wonderful old man called Gelumbhai Patel in Gujerat, who was a devout follower of Mahatma Gandhi. Gandhians cultivate an attitude of non-violence and fearlessness. I will let him tell you his own story.

non-violence in India

'In my work in this remote area of Gujerat, populated only by a few villages of indigenous people, I would often find myself walking for sixty miles through the forest in a day. One day, walking fast, I looked up and saw fifteen feet of stripes and teeth looking at me! It was too late to run, and I was thinking I had had it for sure. I thought to myself, "I wonder what it is like to stroke a tiger?" Instead of walking away, I started to walk towards it!

'Feeling that death was inevitable, I carried on walking closer and closer as the tiger stared at me unblinkingly, and I did wonder why it was taking him so long to jump on me. I thought to myself, "Oh well, I would like my last moments to be meaningful, so here goes, I might as well see what happens." I reached out my hand and patted it on the head!

'Nothing happened! Slowly but surely, a glimmer of hope began to dawn on me. I pulled away my hand and began to walk away from the tiger. I walked and walked and finally reached the edge of the clearing where I slipped quietly into the woods and then ran off as fast as I could – amazed to discover that I was still alive!

'Since then I have had hundreds of encounters with tigers in the forest and never once has any tiger shown any sign of aggression towards me.'

We asked Mr Patel what it was that had enabled him to encounter tigers so peacefully whereas whole villages were living in terror of them and many people had fallen prey to such beasts. His answer reached right into the depths of life's wisdom.

'Gandhi trained us to have no sense of fear or harm in our approach to the people and animals around us. These animals can sense when you mean them harm and they react to that. I approach them with a calm heart and a fearless mind and they never cause me any trouble at all.

'It is in the same way that I can go into areas where there are riots between Muslims and Hindus and speak to the heads of the two communities. They know that I am only there to help, and they listen to me and respect what I have to say.'

Gelumbhai and other Gandhians like him have been instrumental in diffusing riot situations in many towns and cities in India. There is much to be learned from the example of people like Gelumbhai, who are truly living the philsosophy of non-violence and non-aggression and it is having profound effects on the communities in which they live.

We can all live in this way, simply by developing the right attitude to the way we relate to people. Let us all break down the barriers, let go of anger and hatred, and allow the natural love and peacefulness that lies within us to emerge.

Practise awareness. When you become fearful of anything, you are likely to attack in order to defend yourself. If you see something as a threat, you will feel fear. It is therefore useful to be fully aware of your fear and where it comes from.

Watch the fear and ask yourself, 'What can I do?' Then act without regret. Fear cannot be controlled or forced into submission – you have to be brave enough to stand back, watch the fear and then act with its energy. If you can practise acting without regret, you will find your fears will begin to fade away.

AT A GLANCE

MY RELATIONSHIP WITH OTHERS

1   You are the creator of your own life and not the victim. How you perceive a situation will determine the outcome.

2   The world is a mirror of yourself. Seeing agitation around you is a symptom of inner agitation. Look at your negative qualities in a positive way, with gentleness and willingness.

3   Understanding this brings acceptance of the past and the lessons it has given you, for you can never be truly at peace if you hold on to painful memories.

4   Words can heal or destroy so be careful how you use them.

5   What you focus on expands - empower people to be the best that they can be. Give people the space to have their point of view. Respect and love them - focus on the person and the solution, not the problem.

6   Be aware that:
   - every situation is there to teach you something
   - any agitation you feel comes from within
   - if you put yourself in others' shoes, you will understand them better
   - it's important to appreciate and trust people

7   Resolve any negative feelings by letting go of:
   - fear
   - criticism
   - judgement
   - trying to be too perfect

8   Do as you would be done by. Consider how your actions affect others.

'Until the person in front of you means more to you than
your own life, you cannot say that you have truly loved.'

Mahatma Gandhi

UNCONDITIONAL LOVE

unconditional love
a practical approach
listening
living in the moment

Unconditional Love

Unconditional love is a truly remarkable expression of the oneness of life and a powerful expression of the human heart.

Unconditional love that flows freely is the simplest and purest of all acts. This free expression of love only emerges when you can let go of your attachment to and desperation for end results. This not only applies to practical objects, but also to wanting things like love.

If you are not emotionally attached to your doing or being, life is allowed to take its own course. When you are selfless in your inner nature, allowing yourself to flow with the natural laws, then you find you are not interfering with life or trying to make things happen.

In the Pooh Bear stories we can clearly see this unconditional expression. Pooh's uncomplicated and accepting philosophy is simply 'Pooh Is'. All other characters in the story either hesitate or resist the flow of life. Pooh just is.

Unconditional love recognises the perfection of each moment in the same way that Pooh does.

conditional love
Conditional love is full of preoccupation and unnecessary anxiety. Love which is bound by any condition of one kind or another will create intricate complications.

> **If you truly want to lift your heart,**
> **start moving towards an expression of**
> **unconditional love in your life.**

How do I culitivate this love in my life?

slow down
Begin by simply slowing down enough to savour each moment.

respond joyfully
Open yourself to the laughter that is in everything around you, responding to every circumstance with joy.

happy thoughts
Cultivate thoughts that are light-hearted and carefree, and you will begin to experience a natural flow of joy bubbling out from within.

This unconditional uprising of joy is like a song which takes flight on the wings of its own melody, gently settling within the perfect grace of the present moment.

flow with it
But remember - when this surge of unconditional love happens to you, go with it. If you try to control it you may hinder its path, and as these unconditional moments are rare, simply let them flow.

concentration
The ability to concentrate your mind in the here and now is imperative if you want to experience these unconditional outbursts. Concentration on the here and now disconnects you from the past and the future and brings you into the present.

A true encounter with unconditional love has no preferences for extremes such as pain or pleasure, compliments or criticism.

Unconditional love accepts all things as they are.

So an unconditional life implies a future that is free from all boundaries and restrictions.

be patient
In trying to bring about this unconditional way of being, remember to be very patient with yourself and recognise that your mind will struggle with any attempt to change. It may take many years before you can bring it into real focus, for the hungry mind is always grasping. So be aware of this and please be very patient with yourself.

purity

Purity will begin to prevail within you as a long-lasting effect of practising unconditional love, bringing you a new value and depth to life.

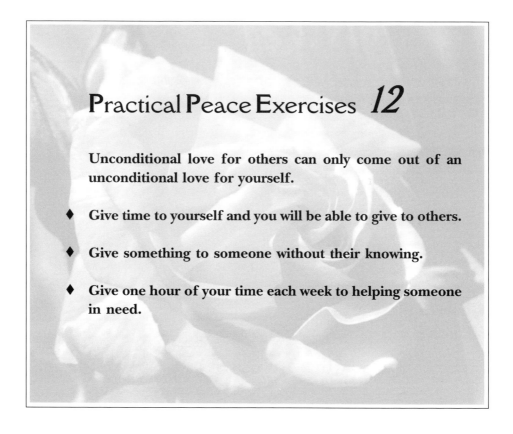

Practical Peace Exercises *12*

Unconditional love for others can only come out of an unconditional love for yourself.

♦ **Give time to yourself and you will be able to give to others.**

♦ **Give something to someone without their knowing.**

♦ **Give one hour of your time each week to helping someone in need.**

UNCONDITIONAL LOVE - A Practical Approach

U nconditional love is about learning to be a source of love instead of waiting for others to love you. People often hesitate to give love, but unconditional love doesn't wait - it jumps in there first!

Like anything else, it requires practice on a regular basis, so I have outlined some ways and means to bring unconditional love alive in your life. Here is a quick check-list you can refer to at any time.

Qualities of Unconditional Love

♦ **accepting yourself**
Relate to other people without fear.
Let go of the need to defend yourself.
Forgive yourself for your imperfections.

♦ **accepting others as they are**
Allow other people to make their own mistakes.
In your expectations of others, try not to be too attached to end results.
Try not to judge or criticise other people's actions.

♦ **tolerance**
Smile inside if someone does something that could be upsetting!
Remain calm - no matter what happens!
Send love to people - not anger.

♦ **forgiveness**
Forgive others for their mistakes and wrong actions.
Try to understand where people are coming from - step into their shoes.
Have a sense of self-responsibility and do not blame others for
things that happen.
Learn to love by putting yourself in a situation that challenges you to
love.
Remember that whatever you give to others, you give to
yourself - so don't hold back!

♦ **separateness**
When you experience barriers or uncomfortable feelings with other people, try to give out more love, both to them and to yourself.

If something hurts you, don't battle with yourself - give love to the situation.

If you can keep your heart open when it hurts, you will discover the treasure of love within that pain.

Remember that the people who appear to be the most unlovable are the ones who need your love the most.

Please remember - unconditional love always jumps in first!
Unconditional love gives and enjoys giving more.
Unconditional love expects nothing in return.
Unconditional love forgives and forgets!

LISTENING

**Listening is like a song -
beautiful, romantic and inspiring.**

Try to walk through life gracefully. If you want to truly appreciate life, walk upon the earth in a sacred way, fearlessly, with complete openness and spontaneity. Don't be too frightened to take the next step just in case it leads into a swamp or quicksand.

Perhaps you need to change your perspective a little bit and open to people in different ways; to honour people and all living things in a way that you have never done before. Savour the moment, considering every discovery and inspiration to be a stepping stone, not a fixed conclusion.

It can begin with the smallest exchange. Talk to people on the street or the people you live with and really give yourself the opportunity to listen to what they have to say.

A good listener has an open heart and a mind that is non-judgemental. Listen in such a complete way that everything is calm and still. Have an attitude of gentle acceptance. Each word is then heard with its true meaning.

**The listener and the speaker become one
and a beautiful dance begins between them.**

Listen attentively to everyone around you, so that people enjoy your listening. Listen closely, and then respond with compassion and grace instead of shyness and fear. Listen to the softness of a voice and its gentleness. Listen to the wisdom and knowledge within that voice - you can hear eternity in the words and feel infinity reaching out from the person who is communicating with you.

Without a listener there can be no speaker, so delight in the experience of listening. The first necessity of learning to love is being able to listen to life itself.

Understand that you can miss the mystery and the magic of each moment by not listening in the right way. Try not to listen with a foregone conclusion in your mind. Hear what is actually being said, not what you would like to hear.

If you take time to listen closely to others and to hear what is being expressed, it can make a dramatic change to your own mind and the way you think. Your whole consciousness can alter, enabling you to touch parts of your being in a totally unique and previously unknown way.

This conscious listening is the beginning of an unconditional loving response - firstly to yourself and secondly to everything that is outside and around you.

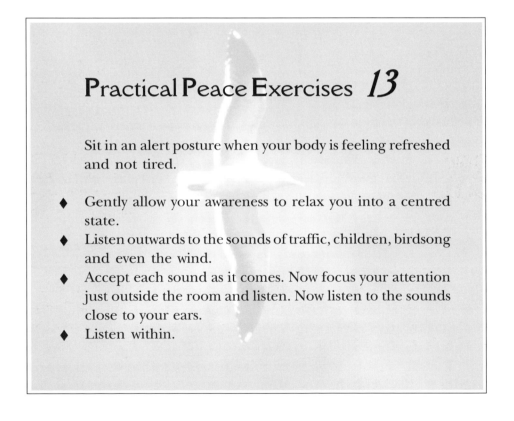

Practical Peace Exercises *13*

Sit in an alert posture when your body is feeling refreshed and not tired.

♦ Gently allow your awareness to relax you into a centred state.

♦ Listen outwards to the sounds of traffic, children, birdsong and even the wind.

♦ Accept each sound as it comes. Now focus your attention just outside the room and listen. Now listen to the sounds close to your ears.

♦ Listen within.

LIVING IN THE MOMENT

J ust saying 'this world needs love', is not enough to make it happen. The fact that you want more peace in your life doesn't make it happen. It's just a starting point from which you begin to wake up. You could decide one day to plant a tree on top of a hill, but just imagine how long it will take for that seedling to grow into a mature tree.

How many circumstances could occur to interrupt the process of its growth? Howling winds and driving rain, moles tunnelling through the roots, lambs trampling and nibbling the seedling. The chances of survival are so remote and yet we see all around us the miracle of trees that have survived for hundreds of years.

It is a miracle, but what about your own story? Ask yourself this question, 'How did I manage to survive with so much perfection?' A time of introspection is a lovely place to start, but I wonder if you can really appreciate this if you rush about too much in your life?

appreciate life
It doesn't mean you have to sit under a tree all day reflecting upon the wonder of life. We are not seeking to cultivate a passive nature, but a stillness and a silence within ourselves. This will enable us to simply appreciate life, not only for what has been so far and what is going to be in the future, but what is in this moment now.

magic moments
I am sure you have experienced moments that have been so perfect, so full of love and inspiration, that you wished you could stay there forever. Have you ever wondered what it is that makes you leave those joy-filled moments?

active participation
The answer is that it takes active participation on your part to make each moment meaningful. It is up to you to search for, and discover, what really lies within this moment now.

treasure each moment

Life can become meaningless if we do not treasure each and every moment. If we fail to enter into life with great sensitivity and attention, our words can become empty and our actions pointless. This only serves to create a sense of sadness within us.

The rest of life can either become scattered with just a few precious moments, or filled with thousands of moments of joy and appreciation for the beauty of being alive. This personal happiness will affect thousands around us - even nations and continents.

this moment is sacred

World peace and the peace of all things actually lies within the sacredness of this moment now. This realisation can only be discovered by each individual from their own experience and understanding of this truth.

---

the precious GIFT of TIME

One day, some animals were talking amongst themselves about what human beings take from them, and a little snail just happened to be passing by. He couldn't resist making a comment on the subject.
'You know,' he said, 'there is something which I have, that human beings would take away from me if they only knew how.'
'What on earth could a tiny creature like you have that human beings would want?' said the other animals in disbelief.
'The one thing that I have is time - I have all the time in the world.'

---

time

Human beings are so caught up in the complexity of life that they are unable to taste the greatest of all treasures which is time itself. People are therefore unable to fully appreciate the power of living from one moment to the next.

Have you ever thought about how abstract time is? It is really just a mental concept that is based upon events of the past, or plans for the future. In reality, time only exists here in the present - not in the past or in the future.

live in the NOW

If someone asked me to design a watch, I would just have the letters NOW printed on it and nothing else! It is because people do not recognise that now is the only time they are given, that they continue to suffer in life.

living one moment at a time

Given that we only have one moment at any one time, we need to participate in that moment with great care and understanding. Then, and only then, will all the forces of life be brought together in a harmonious and balanced symmetry.

> **Like a candle shining equally in all directions,**
> **you have the ability to create a perfect light**
> **in every second that is passing by.**
> **The whole of the mystery of life**
> **is made available to you in this moment.**

become absorbed

Have you ever watched a craftsman at work and noticed that he seems to be in a world of his own, totally absorbed in the detail of his work? He lends depth to his moment-to-moment experience, producing something so beautiful that it is just a miracle.

open to life

Why not give the spirit of life - and yourself - an opportunity to enter a completely new territory, where you don't know quite what is going to happen next, leaving yourself open to whatever life may present.

letting go

Of course this means letting go - of the past with all its fears and phobias, and of future anxiety and worry. It means letting go of what you think you know and of your expectations. It means placing yourself in a territory which has no boundaries or limitations. Then the unexpected is allowed to express itself in a most mysterious and surprising way.

don't limit yourself

Too much of our time during the day is spent within the limitations of our own self-assessment. We predict how capable or incapable we think we are or how efficient our actions will or will not be. We have come to nurture and empower these limitations within ourselves simply by the small fraction of what we know our life to be.

I wonder if you would allow yourself to venture into any other territory beyond these self-imposed limitations?

Your whole day can be spent in the predictability of assumptions and foregone conclusions. Consequently the possibility of a greater truth, a greater reality being born in your life, is annihilated moment by moment.

The moment you think you 'know' something you become comfortable within that knowing, and within that comfort lies the very cage that restricts your ability to transcend your limitations in life.

Your known discoveries can limit and bind you, because you believe you have found all the answers. This leaves you with nothing more to seek out and discover.

Living in the moment is a very beautiful and a very powerful thing. But what are you doing with that moment?

quality time

In the USA recently, a survey was conducted amongst a number of parents to see how much quality time they were actually spending with their children. Microphones were attached to the fathers to observe the communication that took place between them and their children, and the results were astounding. They averaged thirty six seconds of quality communication over a period of six weeks! That was all the time they could find, which indicates that the rest of their time was spent in running around and thinking about how they could spend more time with their children! Doesn't it make you think?

stop rushing around

The restless monkey mind is always saying 'What next? What next?' It never allows you to be here, with yourself and with your life in this moment. Rushing around is something that we have always been encouraged to do and it takes real courage and wisdom to raise your hand and say, 'Stop! This moment now - the one I am in - is all that matters.'

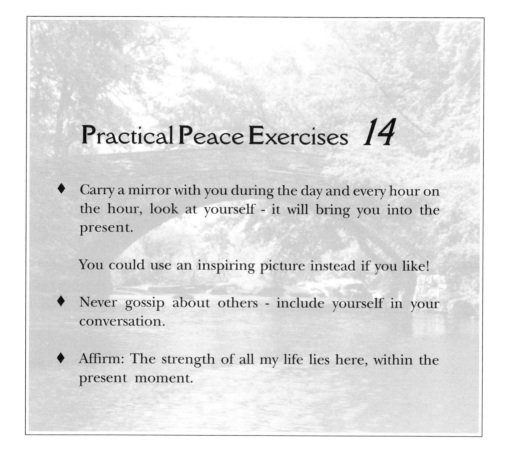

Practical Peace Exercises *14*

♦ Carry a mirror with you during the day and every hour on the hour, look at yourself - it will bring you into the present.

You could use an inspiring picture instead if you like!

♦ Never gossip about others - include yourself in your conversation.

♦ Affirm: The strength of all my life lies here, within the present moment.

AT A GLANCE

UNCONDITIONAL LOVE

1   Unconditional love is one of the most powerful expressions of the human heart.

2   Let go of attachment to doing and being and especially to end results.

3   Take hold of:
- Pooh Bear philosophy
- joyful responses and happy thoughts
- flowing with life and being patient

4   Always remember - unconditional love doesn't wait; it jumps in there first!

5   The first necessity of learning to love is being able to listen to life itself. Walk through life gracefully, in a sacred way.

6   Listen to people and really try to hear what they have to say.

7   Live in the moment - let go of:
- the past and the future
- rushing around
- fears and phobias
- foregone conclusions

Eurowalk 2000 - North Wales

UNITY AND ONENESS

friendship
unity
unity in action
oneness

FRIENDSHIP

True friendship is one of the most precious things in life. Can you imagine a life without people to share your tears and laughter, your deepest thoughts and feelings? Loneliness does not feel natural or right but we have to realise that lasting friendship is not a passive exercise; it requires our active participation to make it flourish.

An agitated mind has no time for anyone, but a person who has a calm, contented mind will always find time for people who appear on their doorstep.

I wonder if life has any meaning or purpose if we cannot welcome and love people in this way. No amount of wealth or knowledge can satisfy us if we remain isolated from our fellow human beings. The world needs peace and friendship in order to solve its problems; it is only by working collectively that we will be able to achieve this.

The true basis of lasting friendship is one that draws upon this truth in life and the feeling of the human heart is the most practical tool that can guide us.

resolve
For friendship to happen we need to have a resolve that we are going to make it happen, firstly within ourselves and then with the people around us.

giving
We have to give of ourselves in order to form a creative, flowing experience between people. Giving is such a beautiful thing and an essential part of friendship. Whatever we give, spirals out into the universe - and beyond. Like throwing a pebble into a lake, the ripples extend out endlessly. Every single act of friendship creates a powerful thought process that echoes around the whole world, even if it is only making someone a cup of tea, or massaging their shoulders when they are tired.

94

selflessness

To understand more deeply the nature of giving, consider the quality of selflessness. Living selflessly means you have as much concern for others as you do for yourself. The famous St Francis prayer says:

> **May I never seek so much to be consoled**
> **as to console, to be loved as to love,**
> **for it is in giving that we receive.**

There is such a profound truth within these simple words - a truth that can set us free. What is special to all the great teachers like St Francis or Mahatma Gandhi is their quality of selfless giving. They discovered that when you put as much energy into giving as you do into trying to receive, a beautiful sense of oneness is born in your life.

Selflessness is another name for oneness, because when we can forget ourselves we become a part of the greater whole. We begin to feel genuine care and concern for our human family, which means every other human being.

> **Acknowledging the oneness of all life cements the foundation**
> **for a true global family.**

The heart of friendship lies in the recognition of the oneness of all things and the common love within us all. When we can recognise the peace that lies within our own hearts, true friendship will evolve naturally. That peace will spiral and expand outwards. World peace is then an inevitable result.

BEAR cub

There is a lovely story about a mother polar bear and her little cub. One day the cub came to its mother and asked her, 'Mum, am I really a polar bear?'

'Of course you are, little one, look at your beautiful white fur, just like mine.'

The next day the cub came to its mother and asked the same

question to which she replied, 'Yes, look at your nose and your whiskers. What else could you be?'

The next day the little cub said, 'Mum, are you sure I am not a koala bear, or a grizzly bear?'

'Son,' replied the mother, 'why do you keep asking me these strange questions? Why don't you believe you are a polar bear?'

'Because I'm cold!' said the little bear.

The mother embraced her little cub and he soon became warm again.

friendship in Uganda

A senior employee in the forestry commission in Uganda went through school as a child with two great and dear friends. They were inseparable. After they left school, each went to a different university; one of his friends went to study politics and the other finance.

He saw them very rarely after that, but now they are very much a part of his life again. The friend who studied political science became the President of Uganda and the other who studied finance has become the Ugandan Treasurer. Both were responsible for pulling Uganda out of Africa's worst social turmoil and back into the world's community of nations.

You just never know who or what your friends will become! Friendship deserves our greatest respect, for if we honour people, they will always be our friends - if we don't, we may lose them.

trust

If you can truly appreciate and honour people when you are with them, trust will develop naturally. Dissolve those thoughts and expressions that create boundaries between you and the rest of the world. Wouldn't it be wonderful if in every situation, with every person, circumstance or predicament you could experience life as a flow between people? If you and I can do it individually we can do it collectively.

**It is important to anchor respect for people
so that you are full of gratitude
for their presence in your life.**

Practical Peace Exercises *15*

♦ The next time you are with some friends, just enjoy being in their company without any expectations

♦ Enjoy the moments of happiness or sadness, laughter or tears.

♦ Simply appreciate them for being in your life.

'Even as drops of water make the ocean,
so we too, through friendship,
can become an ocean of friendliness.
The shape of the world would indeed be transformed
if all of us lived in a spirit of love and amity
with one another.'

Mahatma Gandhi

UNITY

E cology and modern global issues demonstrate that all of life is intricately interconnected. Each one of us is a part of various dynamic, living systems made up of many individuals - our family, our workplace, our society and our world.

These systems work best when all their parts are co-operating symbiotically. Can you imagine a system where the components argue and fight?

PECKING order

The Senses all lived together in a little house called Human Body. Each one of them considered themselves to be the most important being in that house. The rivalry built up so much between them that they decided to have a competition to see which Sense was in fact the most important.

So one day Hearing decided to leave for a whole day. Everything managed to function perfectly well without him, much to his disappointment. The next day Sight left and although it was a bit dark, everything kept going normally. Then Smell and Touch left with the same result. But when Breath left everyone panicked and begged him to come back straight away, for they knew they could not survive without him!

---

create a symphony
We are all like members of an orchestra, each having our own instrument and part to play. No one is better than another and if we play together in harmony, we create a beautiful symphony. Trying to play our own tune without listening to everyone else just makes a terrible noise and doesn't get anybody anywhere!

Human experience has shown that systems or groups that are the most unified, are the most productive, harmonious, happy, efficient, fulfilled and durable. They are more able to withstand and indeed grow from inner conflict and diversity. These are evidently desirable goals, so how do we achieve them?

Before we can answer that question, it will be necessary to examine the most fundamental and intriguing question of all time.

What is the purpose of life?

This enquiry actually contains within itself everything that you are, everything that you believe you are and everything that you would like to become.

Initially you may not find the question very attractive or even important, but before your mind switches off and thinks of other things, just hold on a moment! Let's see where it takes us, because it might reveal some fundamental answers.

This particular question drives us on each day to work so hard, with much effort, time and planning. We are constantly busy acquiring and disposing of wealth and possessions. We do so many different things to try to justify our presence in this life.

Rather than constantly side-stepping the issue and dealing only with the trivial things of life, I wonder if it might not be wiser to spend a bit more time in seeking the answer to this basic question? Can we really dare to get to the core of the matter?

search deeply

Do you sometimes feel lonely, isolated, confused or unhappy? If so, perhaps you have not searched deeply enough for the answer to this mystery. It is possible you have never persisted in looking for the answer in a tangible and practical way. If your life has gone by very rapidly and the last ten to sixty years have just drifted past, then I wonder if it is possible that you have not stayed still long enough in one place to discover the purpose of your life?

The purpose of life is unity.

Once again we are brought full circle by the spinning wheel of life - back to our common purpose which is to create unity and harmony in everything we do and with everyone we meet.

How can you become a person in whose presence things just come together in a unified and harmonious way? Regardless of the role we play in life, we all need to awaken and learn how to create a synthesis so that unity may evolve in our world.

join with others
Bringing unity into our lives and into this world is a function of more than one person. Whenever we isolate ourselves from others, we will have problems. If you were the only human being on this planet, there would be no need for peace because you would have no-one to fight with and nothing to fight for.

People sometimes like to believe that life is about separateness, but if you say, 'I am separate from you,' you will experience problems, because if separation is your foundation, you will never experience a sense of union with others.

Imagine a river splitting itself into two separate paths and saying to the other half of the water, 'Don't flow with me, I want to do it on my own.' There would simply be no sense to it.

the way of nature
We were made to be with others - that is the way it is meant to be. There should be oneness with all peoples, north, south, east and west. That is why when you join with others, it creates such a beautiful feeling within you - and simply feels right.

So the challenge that we have in bringing peace into our lives and into this world, is to become willing to participate with people and events around us in a way that is accepting, spontaneous and regenerating.

If we accept that peace is a function of many and not just an isolated few, we have no choice; we have to bring the many into the one.
It is the coming together of the divided parts of the complete whole that brings unity and peace.

co-operation

Have you ever watched a flock of geese in flight? The way they fly together is a perfect depiction of unity. There is a common purpose - the first one breaks the current of air and takes the impact, which enables the others to work less hard. After about two or three miles another goose will take the lead and in this way they are able to fly for hundreds of miles. Can you imagine what would happen if one of them refused to do it?

You will only have unity where there is co-operation.

the common cause

Where there is a common cause, there will be unity within that cause and that very unity is the factor that brings success. Our common cause is our mutual concern for our planet and all its creatures. We are now being called forth to become true friends of the earth, but
let us make friends with each other first.

world leaders in Rio de Janeiro

At the Earth Summit, we all witnessed history in the making when the assembled world presidents and politicians from every nation posed for the first group photograph in the history of mankind. What was it that brought together these leaders in such an expression of, and quest for, consensus on their world's environmental and developmental problems?

It was the culmination of the work of countless concerned people who for the previous thirty years and more had been constantly caring, campaigning and working for the environment.

**Never doubt that the small things
we do as individuals
in the end do change the world.**

having fun in Hungary

In Hungary the largest non-governmental organisation to plant trees makes sure that tree planting is fun, calling in the local folk band, bringing in volunteer caterers and inviting thousands of people to come. They hand everyone a tree to plant and invite them to take part in a folk festival. By the end of the day several thousand trees are planted amidst a wonderful atmosphere of joy and celebration. In addition there is a lot of money raised in donations to the organisation.

People just love to have fun when they are changing the world.

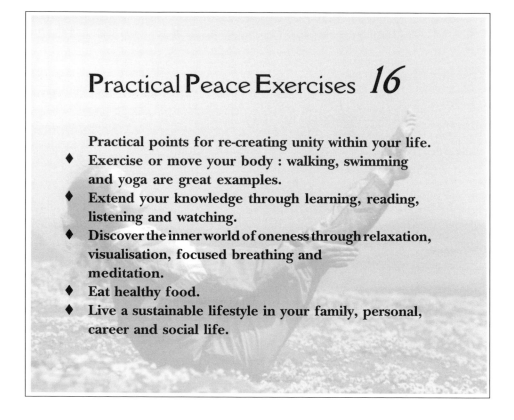

Practical Peace Exercises *16*

Practical points for re-creating unity within your life.
- ◆ **Exercise or move your body : walking, swimming and yoga are great examples.**
- ◆ **Extend your knowledge through learning, reading, listening and watching.**
- ◆ **Discover the inner world of oneness through relaxation, visualisation, focused breathing and meditation.**
- ◆ **Eat healthy food.**
- ◆ **Live a sustainable lifestyle in your family, personal, career and social life.**

'Of a certainty, the man who can see all ceatures in himself
and himself in all creatures, knows no sorrow.'

Anon

UNITY IN ACTION

Mother Teresa's home

When I was in India I had the enormous privilege of spending some time at Mother Teresa's home in Calcutta. On one particular afternoon I looked out from the balcony and noticed the Sisters of Charity working together in the most exquisite way.

They were passing buckets of water to each other from an outside tap, and up some steps to the first floor. It was like watching waves on the ocean rising and falling, cascading into gentleness and strength - like a beautiful dance unfolding. I could see the delight in their eyes, the strength in their arms and the dance in their feet as they tried to get to the next sister as quickly as possible in order to help to make her burden lighter.

Having passed the bucket on, they then tried to get back quickly to the sister on their other side so that she wouldn't have to walk too far either. It was quite touching to see the way they worked together and the wonderful grace and joy they created in their unity.

These sisters do not work for money or power, but simply for the joy of service and their common cause and it is obvious they have discovered that there is love within action and a connectedness in that love which unites everything.

I know that everyone who witnessed this scene was profoundly affected and that image will certainly be implanted in my own heart for ever. It completely encapsulates the beauty of the human spirit and the harmony of oneness.

There is so much to be learned from these wonderful sisters, for we too can bring great joy and enthusiasm into everything we do, with an awareness of something much deeper, higher and more noble than just simply doing an action for its own sake.

It is said that the power of a nation is achieved by the coming together or union of its people. One stick on its own can be broken, but put twenty together and you cannot break them.

It is the same with a human being. When the body, mind and senses are focused on the same goal, that is precisely the point from which peace can be born, and it is at that point that we can find a place of utter calmness - a place where we can rest and which we can call our home.

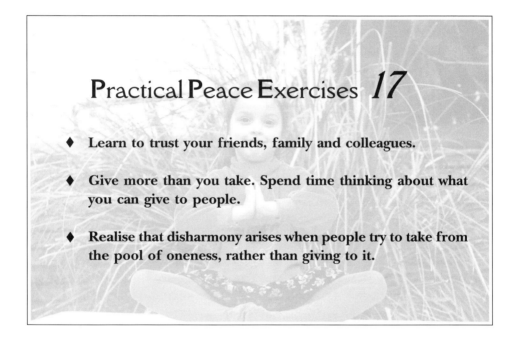

Practical Peace Exercises *17*

♦ **Learn to trust your friends, family and colleagues.**

♦ **Give more than you take. Spend time thinking about what you can give to people.**

♦ **Realise that disharmony arises when people try to take from the pool of oneness, rather than giving to it.**

'One of the basic points is kindness.
With kindness, with love and compassion,
with this feeling that is the
essence of brotherhood and sisterhood,
one will have inner peace.
This compassionate feeling is the basis of inner peace.'

The Dalai Lama

ONENESS

Just for a moment, imagine that you are an iceberg - a massive, frozen entity, suspended by infinite volumes of water, floating, isolated and alone. The great expanse of the ocean seems to emphasise your solitude as it stretches out endlessly in all directions.

The water around you feels warm, but you feel totally cold inside. Imagine the loneliness you feel as you float, ice-bound and separate, unable to move. Imagine the longing you feel simply to melt into the warmth of the ocean.

Imagine suddenly realising that you are made up of the same water as the ocean - what a realisation! So how then do we change from this frozen, isolated state into a state of oneness with the ocean? Isn't it just a matter of becoming warmer inside?

What happens when we 'warm' towards someone? A connection is made and the barriers start to melt away. Unity is developing.

The very first principle which I personally think is crucial to the peace and well-being of all living things, is the recognition that all life is one. If you stand still long enough in your life to look at everything that is living, moving and breathing, you will begin to notice that everything is flowing into everything else. There is an interconnect-edness and a continuity with the whole of life. We are all connected to one another and to every living thing - every blade of grass and every drop of rain.

This interconnectedness includes the animals roaming in the forests, the creatures inhabiting the depths of the oceans and the birds flying so freely in the sky. It includes mountain ranges, lakes, trees and the earth itself with all its minerals and amazing substances which sustain and enhance our lives.

Awareness of this oneness imparts a sense of freedom and love, which can totally remove fear from our lives. Fear makes it difficult for us to deal with life effectively. It stems from a past that makes us feel weak, and a future that renders us incapable of focusing upon and achieving our ambitions.

fear
The only thing that really separates people from each other and from oneness is the limited mind that tells us we are all alone in a hostile world and need to defend ourselves. Fear is probably one of the main things that sabotage our success in life. Past regrets and an uncertain future rob us of our security in the present and so we feel the need for accumulation and greed.

exploitation
The natural outcome of fear is exploitation. We begin to feel that the only answer is to accumulate as much as possible to provide for the uncertain future that lies ahead, but only because we are not able to feel safe and happy in the present. Great leaders of peace like Mahatma Gandhi, Martin Luther King and even St Francis of Assisi, have demonstrated the practicality of living a life without fear and greed. As Gandhi used to say, 'There is enough for everyone's need, but not for everyone's greed.'

The lives of these great men and women demonstrate very clearly that if we can replace qualities such as fear and greed with other all-embracing qualities like love and generosity, then human beings can begin to find a new dimension in their lives and experience something much more profound than the accumulation of wealth.

What is the nature of the limited mind that creates thoughts of separation and acts of exploitation?

the mind
We often tend to limit the mind to the brain, but scientists today are proving that there are brain cells throughout the whole body. Does that mean that the mind flows throughout your whole body? I would like to suggest that it does.

living mind in motion
Every white blood cell in your body contains the same tissue as the brain, which means that those blood cells are one living brain in motion! A

living mind in motion. Now doesn't that challenge the reality of where your mind really is?

We tend to see each mind as separate and divided and never coming together. If we want to experience something greater, it is vital to realise that the real mind does not work within the limitations of time and space.

out of time and space
How is it that you often think of someone you haven't seen for years and then they ring you up or a letter arrives out of the blue? It is because our minds are all connected and the universal mind works outside of time. There are hundreds of incidents occurring every single day to prove that the mind is absolutely everywhere!

You could be so busy living within the confines of the limited mind, planning out tomorrow, that you could actually miss the whole of your life. The consciousness of the all-pervading mind does not dwell in tomorrow or next week, but in the here and now.

FROG in the WELL

There once was a little frog who lived in a deep, dark well. He loved his home and spent many happy hours swimming round and round and round it. One day, another frog hopped into the well and said to the first frog, 'Hey, do you know there is an incredible world out there beyond this well?'
'What do you mean?' said the first frog.
'Well, there are birds and trees, an enormous expanse of blue sky, mountains and rivers, streams and oceans, much, much bigger than this well. Why don't you come with me and see for yourself?'
'No,' said the little frog, 'I know that this well is the whole universe - there is nothing else.'
Nothing could persuade him otherwise and so the visiting frog sadly left him, to swim round and round and round...

To return to the original oneness of life we need to expand the parameters of our mind into the universal mind. Until every human being can recognise their innate connectedness, there can never be unity and the secret lies in seeing the oneness in everything and everyone.

think oneness

As thought is one of the most important vehicles through which we express ourselves in the world, we need to ask ourselves:

> - Do my thoughts create oneness or separation?
> - Do my thoughts create love or hatred?
> - Do my thoughts create trust or mistrust?

If you want to move into an experience of oneness, begin by allowing your thoughts to create peace and love, acknowledging your connection to everything, and having respect for all beings.

Oneness also means having compassion for the animals that roam on the earth, the creatures that live in the depths of the ocean and the birds that fly in the air. They share the oneness too, so we have an added responsibility towards them.

In terms of the oneness, the lowest animal and the highest man are the same. This became very clear to the FWF team on a flight from Uganda across Zaire. Looking down over the African jungle, they could see no difference between the highest tree and the lowest, between the grassland and the forest. It all appeared the same.

If there are differences in the world they are in degree, not in kind. Differences between people are about differences of expression - for everyone has the same basic aspirations.

melting the iceberg

In our isolation and separateness we can become frozen - and this creates so many problems. It is necessary to have an intense desire to melt the barriers of separation that we have created between us, in order to allow the experience of union - of unity - to happen.

Any wise being will tell you that unity is the way towards peace; that coming together - merging together - is the only way to harmony and peace for all living beings.

the oneness habit

In your everyday life build the oneness habit of blessing and appreciating life rather than judging and condemning it. Neither should there be any regrets about mistakes of the past, only gratitude for all that has happened and brought us to this point in our life. So no matter what challenges you face, understand that all will be well in the end.

The single most important factor in oneness is the ability to have compassion. When this quality is present in our every thought, word and deed, it will bring oneness.

There is something so fine, so regal about us all.
Let us recognise this inner beauty
and the life that connects us all together
and celebrate it, together!

Prioritise activities in your life that allow you to experience the reality of oneness. Simple acts like feeding the birds, planting a tree, standing on the earth, raising your arms to the sky and greeting the sun - are all ways to connect with the oneness of life.

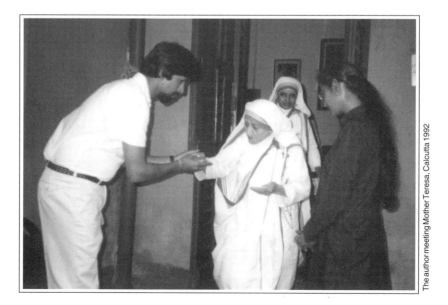

The author meeting Mother Teresa, Calcutta 1992

Practical Peace Exercises *18*

♦ **Visualise your friends, family and colleagues and mentally say to each one of them in turn, 'You and I are the same - both part of the oneness of life.'**
♦ **Every morning feed the birds.**
♦ **Touch the earth whenever you can and feel your connection to it.**
♦ **Nurture thoughts that create oneness, thoughts that lead to harmony, thoughts that create love, trust and friendship.**
♦ **Be compassionate to all. Do not exploit the earth - wear natural fibres and eat natural food.**
♦ **Plant trees whenever and wherever you can!**

'Works of love are always works of peace.
The more we share with each other,
the more there will be love, unity and compassion.
And we will be able to spread the
joy of loving wherever we go.'

Mother Teresa

AT A GLANCE

FRIENDSHIP, UNITY & ONENESS

1   Most people live in isolation and feel separate from each other like an iceberg. How can we experience unity and oneness?

2   By seeking re-unity at every opportunity.

3   It is crucial that our interactions are positive, unity - building, open and free from agitation and resistance.

4   Whenever we isolate ourselves we create problems - don't be an iceberg!

5   The world needs friendship in order to solve the great problems of our time because they can only be solved collectively. The foundation of friendship is *Truth*.

6   Creating a friendship adventure:
- trust the intuition of your heart
- open to the love that you are
- discover the oneness that links every heart
- listen to the call of the heart

7   Experience the oneness in all things:
- feed the birds every morning
- take time to feel your connection to nature
- plant trees, bulbs and flowers

'A successful human being is one who
is content within himself and with his life,
as it is - NOW.'

Mansukh

EQUATION FOR SUCCESS

five steps to self-empowerment
commitment to change
the power of the here and now
the power of gratitude
the power of generosity
your personal dreams

THE FIVE STEPS to SELF-EMPOWERMENT

S uccess means different things to different people. To one person it may be making a lot of money or having a thriving business. To another, it may be having wonderful relationships with family and friends and to another, feeling very happy and carefree without any responsibilities in this world.

We all aspire to success and happiness and if we care to take a close look behind the scenes of the lives and personalities of individuals who have achieved outstanding success in any sphere of their lives, we will discover a common thread. The beautiful thing about that 'special something' is that it is within the reach of each and every one of us - regardless of our circumstances in life.

I would like to offer you these 'Five Steps to Self-Empowerment' which constitute that 'special something'. If you can uphold and live by these five principles whatever your endeavour may be - you will always be successful in your life.

To achieve anything in life that is worthwhile, we always have two options.

We can either achieve success through a beautiful, organic process which complements everyone around us, and still takes us to our goal. Or we can compete with aggression and false pride and a 'come what may I will get there' attitude. This attitude often involves a senseless onslaught of fear, anger, denials and hurt and an unnecessary destruction of everything that stands in our way.

Since the choice lies with us, it is only right and proper that we decide the optimum route to harmony and growth. One of the goals which is innate to all living beings is the desire to share a common destiny and openly trust each other on the journey of successful living.

If you ask someone how they are, or how their career is doing, you are often met with a tirade of problems. Not enough money coming in to pay the mortgage, or too many challenges at home - the list can be endless.

Sometimes your home life is good, but your career lies in tatters, or your career is going well but your health is suffering. Children and family may be happy, but we are totally exhausted and drained by life. We work so hard and are left unable to enjoy the rewards of our work, due to lack of time, energy or health.

We have been told for many years that a successful human being is one who is incredibly dynamic. He or she goes abroad four times a week and has twenty business meetings a day. We are led to believe that a successful person is one who gets so much done. People are always rushing around everywhere, but do they know where they are going?

I would like to suggest that a successful human being is one who is content within himself and with his life, as it is now - unconditionally. When you actually uncover your peaceful nature, life will just fall into place. Success is inevitable. As long as your priority in life is to be calm, content and peaceful, everything will work - right across the board.

The first thing to remember is that the time to begin is right now - in this present moment and exactly where you find yourself today. Life does not repeat itself - it is ever fresh.

1 COMMITMENT TO CHANGE

**You cannot discover new oceans
unless you have the courage to lose sight of the shore.**

Life gives back to you whatever you put into it. If your commitment is small your results will be small. If it is deep the results will be significant and meaningful.

Change is a constant ingredient for growth. The greatest changes in life take place when you are actively involved in living - totally engaged in it moment by moment, flowing with all that life presents to you, because life changes when you change.

resistance

A resolution to change will often be met by resistance from your inner conditioning, and this can be a real challenge. For example, you resolve to save money this week and you lose your purse. You decide to give up sugar and everyone comes round with boxes of chocolates or cream cakes. Your inner conditioning will always tend to resist your growth towards change - initially. The part of you that wants to stay the same will always fight, so just remember this and when you feel the resistance, hang on long enough for it to let go.

risk

The word risk is a password for miracles and the most important thing to remember about taking a risk is that it does not involve guess-work. It requires putting your deepest thoughts and feelings into practice. This means you have to trust yourself.

trust

Ask yourself if there is a discrepancy between what you say and what you do. Confront yourself. Think about it carefully, and be honest in your reply. Learn to trust yourself in what you say and do, and don't ever regret any decision you make. The more you can trust yourself, the greater the power behind your actions.

persistence

There is an immense power within you that wants to check out the sincerity of your resolve to change. This is a very important natural law. When you persist in your resolve to change and actually prove to that inner power that you are serious, all the doors open wide for you.

the law of grace

Once you make a solid commitment to change, you are giving sanction to yourself to start moving with the Law of Grace in your life. Grace is that mysterious phenomenon that we do not quite understand. It is responsible for the miracles that occur every day under your very nose which you sometimes notice and other times do not.

Grace picks you up each morning and delivers you safe and well at the end of the day, because so many things could happen to you in just one day.

A friend of mine once had a brass ornament on her mantelpiece which had been there for over thirty years. She used to polish it lovingly every day and her children used to play with it regularly. One day a visitor noticed this object and asked if she would mind if he had it examined. She had no objections, but was very surprised to discover that it was in fact an unexploded shell from the first World War. Can you imagine the grace that must have been moving in her life for all those years?

Grace is also that special energy which allows our endeavours to be successful. Here is just one example that the FWF team came across in Belgium.

Gandhian worker in Brussels
Georges is a tireless Gandhian worker who, after many years working on Gandhian issues, resolved to create a newsletter. This resolution was made despite the fact that at that time he had no savings and was unemployed.

That same day a friend called by with the offer of a typewriter, and the next day someone he had not contacted for years rang to see if Georges knew anyone who could use a printing press! The following week a company offered a plentiful supply of paper and the Gandhi Centre newsletter is now one of the most established Gandhian journals throughout Europe. In your own life it is a great adventure to look for the signs of miracles like these - the 'little coincidences' that assist you during the day. Carl Jung calls them 'synchronisities'. You will see them everywhere and then you become aware that there is something very powerful on your side in life. This awareness puts you in touch with the truth in life, the reality of your existence.

When you start to live in conscious awareness of the Law of Grace, you will find it much easier to trust life. The knowledge that the universe is on your side gives you a deep sense of trust and safety. Fear no longer predominates in your life and risks become much easier to take.

Australian peace worker

Margaret is a Quaker peacemaker who is seventy years old and blind. The thing that is so special about her is that she has dedicated her life to the service of others. During the time of some bushfires in Tasmania she spent all her time visiting people, offering help, providing counselling and support, as well as opening her door to anyone and everyone. She made a point of visiting all the villages and homesteads to counsel people in shock.

When she heard there was someone living in a caravan on her own, many miles out in the wilds, she travelled through torrential rain to reach her. When she arrived at the caravan there was no reply to her knock, so she just spoke a few comforting words at the door and left.

Many months later, Margaret was approached by a woman who told her that she had actually saved her life, although they had never met. She explained that she was the person who lived in that isolated caravan and that when Margaret had knocked on the door that rainy day, she was about to take her own life. Those few, loving words spoken through a closed door had touched her enough to prevent her from taking that step.

That is grace in action - the force of goodness that moves in all our lives. When you can learn to trust that grace, and move with it, it is like sailing downstream and your life becomes effortless being.

2 THE POWER OF THE HERE AND NOW

Have you ever thought what it is that takes you away from the power of living one moment at a time? Here are three factors you might like to consider:

- condemning people unnecessarily
- worrying about the past and the future
- fighting the flow of your life

live in the moment

Try to stay in the moment. Give your very best to each moment and a tremendous power and energy will start to gently overflow from within you. It is actually indescribable - and once you have discovered it you can start to utilise that deep reservoir of energy creatively.

creativity, courage, spontaneity

If you can live in the moment with intensity, creativity rises up from within and says, 'do this', courage says, 'go for it' and spontaneity enables you to do it. Now the power to direct the course of your life becomes available to you.

learn from your actions

If you do something which tells you nothing about yourself, then it was not worth doing. So make a resolve that whatever you do will teach you something about yourself.

improve your relationships

Then consider that whatever you do should always improve your relationship with others. If you meet opposition in what you are trying to do, see it as a positive sign! Adversity is a very good sign that you are moving in the right direction.

**Remember that the kite of success
generally rises against the wind of adversity.**

intuition

Have the strength of your convictions to follow your inner feelings. Sometimes you may have to stand your ground and trust your intuition, but trust is always a two-way process. Having established your inner strength remember to utilise your wisdom by showing kindness, concern and compassion in your relationships with others.

Australian Aboriginals

One of the most poignant experiences the Eurowalk team had was meeting with the Aboriginal people in Australia where a wonderful youth leader called Raymond Walker drove us across the traditional lands of his tribe - the Nunukul people.

He talked about his people who had walked across the 'Great Southern Land' possibly more than 100,000 years ago. For all these millenia they lived peacefully in the eternal now or 'dream-time', cultivating a deep and profound respect for the Earth.

The traditional Aboriginal way of life may no longer be appropriate to the white people, but their way of living and being has much to teach us and their Ancient Dreaming life is full of answers for a troubled world.

Their message to humanity is, 'Try to live from your heart - reside in the heart - decide with the heart, and then let the mind put your decisions into place.'

Try to appreciate the value of each moment in your life and the power of living in that moment.

3 THE POWER OF GRATITUDE

Most people never even think about the power of gratitude but it is the most simple and natural approach to successful living. It is so simple that people tend to miss it completely.

Just how grateful are you for what life has given you? If you could surround all your thoughts with gratitude, you would not be able to walk around without a huge smile on your face and in your heart.

active participation
When a lightness comes to your heart, your eyes begin to shine, and the result is the kind of laughter and inner freedom that you see in children. People who are grateful in life carry with them the freshness of hope and positive anticipation. They are active participants in life and not passive observers.

Just as a snowdrop contains an essential warmth within its centre in order to survive the winter, so can you glimpse and capture the lasting energy of gratitude to carry you through the trials and tribulations of life's challenges.

gratitude transforms
If you can open your mind with an attitude of pure gratitude every day, you will find that all your experiences will become transformed. The energy of gratitude has the power to change a negative experience into one that is filled with positivity and hope.

express gratitude freely
The Law of Gratitude states that a willingness to express gratitude externally creates a positive feedback, so start by openly expressing gratitude for everything in your life. Learn to appreciate simple things, like the song of a bird, the colours of autumn leaves and the changing seasons.

appreciate everything
Express your thankfulness for a healthy body and mind, for your family and friends and for the food you eat. Try to train your mind towards thoughts of appreciation for everything in your life.

Soon you will find that you are even able to feel grateful for the things in life that feel uncomfortable to you, for expressing gratitude openly will enable you to experience the depth of life in a way you never previously thought possible.

The way you feel will begin to change and before you know it, thoughts like, 'Oh, not another day,' will have altered to, 'It is so good to be alive', almost without your noticing.

attitude
Success in life is totally dependent upon an attitude of mind. When negative thoughts appear to surround you like enemies, it is often hard to imagine how to change them into positive, enlivening ones. Gratitude does it for you! It enables you to see only the best in every situation.

practice brings self-trust
As you practise gratitude, hope and positivity begin to arise in everything you do and you will find that you begin to trust yourself. Trusting in your own capabilities will create a strength of conviction within you that will

enable you to rely on your own resources more and more.

Just sit still long enough and you will begin to see the magic of your life and how much there is to be grateful for. A grateful heart completely understands the qualities of sharing and giving and then the connection between the Law of Gratitude and the Law of Generosity begins to become apparent to you.

4 THE POWER OF GENEROSITY

goodness

Everything which is born and lives comes to an end within a span of time, but there is one human attribute that never ends, and that is goodness. It is the ability to do good. You exhibit this quality when you share yourself with people, in whatever way - your home or food, your clothes or your money, or your time and energy.

boomerang effect

One kind word or action born out of goodness will never die, it just keeps on growing. When you give something away with love, you become a part of the energy of generosity. It is like joining a natural cycle, so that whatever you give has to come back to you, like a boomerang.

When you give away five pounds to a worthy cause, double the energy comes back to you. No-one knows why, but it happens every time. It is almost as though someone 'up there' has an enormous computer which monitors everything that happens in your life!

giving energy

All the centres I have developed began with my giving six hours a week to children with disabilities. This was time taken out of my university studies, but I knew that by giving time and energy, something sustainable was being formed. I started teaching free yoga classes at university and four hundred students came every week! Instead of asking for money for the class, I suggested to people that they could give something to charity, so that they would benefit from the Law of Generosity. From those classes I formed some of the deepest and most lasting friendships of my life. Many of those friends are living and working with me today.

on the move
The energy of life is constantly in motion and when you give something you become a part of that energy. It can be just a little extra effort - a little time, or money, or even just a word of kindness to someone who needs it. Acts of kindness and generosity actually create an end to suffering and will enrich your life beyond measure.

a word of caution
Please do not chase power and fame because it is only in giving that we receive and are able to experience the fullness of what life really has to offer.

My mother used to say, 'If you knew the power of giving, you would not let a plate of food go by without sharing it.' Please take time to reflect on this statement and to absorb its meaning.

giving spontaneously
Spontaneous giving is the most powerful aspect of generosity. You know those times when you just get a feeling you want to give something away but it seems irrational? My advice to you is to DO IT - before your mind comes in and tells you why you should not do it. If you can capture those moments you will release a powerful force for prosperity and success in your life.

5 THE POWER OF YOUR PERSONAL DREAMS

We gravitate towards whatever we think about the most. Therefore, think only of what you want to achieve in your life!

Remember the story of the wish-fulfilling tree that I mentioned in the first chapter? Your whole life is actually a wish-fulfilling tree and everything you project out from yourself really does come into being. Therefore, it is important to think only about what you want to happen, simply because that is what will happen.

So how can you put this principle into practice so that it becomes an advantage to you and not a disadvantage?

tune in
When you sit in meditation, you can tune into the wave-length you want your life to be on. You can begin to become so focused that you direct your thoughts exactly where you want them to go, to attract the right people, places and things into your life.

the power of attraction
You know that feeling when you think of someone and they ring, or a letter drops through the letterbox? It's not just a coincidence - it is actually your birthright that this kind of event should occur for you in every single moment of the day; but it may not happen as fast as you would like it to!

source of power
The power we are talking about is a subconscious one, and this is a very important thing to recognise. It is not a vague phenomenon, but a tangible and inevitable fact. In his book *The Magic of Believing*, Claude Bristol says, 'Just as the conscious mind is a source of benefit, so the subconscious mind is a source of power.'

imagination
Albert Einstein once said that 'imagination is more important than knowledge. At the age of twelve, Leonardo da Vinci used to tell his mother that he would become one of the greatest artists the world had ever known. He constantly imagined himself dressed as an artist and dreamed it constantly, with the result that he actually became one. Neil Armstrong would sit at home visualising himself riding moonbeams. In his imagination he used to affirm that he was going to be the first man on the moon.

So start by dreaming your dreams, which is the mental rehearsal and remember that what you expect, you get! Then you must empower your dreams with actions that are energised by the Law of Generosity. It is one thing to dream your dreams and quite another to act upon them. Just a personal suggestion at this point - when something works, please try and use it first - and figure it out later!

Practical Peace Exercise *19*

COMMITMENT TO CHANGE

- ♦ Think of an attribute you wish to change and practise introspection.
- ♦ Begin the process by replacing the negative qualities with their polar opposites.
- ♦ Cultivate the habit of imagining the person you want to become and then commitment will arise as naturally as the sun rises in the morning.

THE POWER OF THE HERE AND NOW

- ♦ Spend time working in a cancer centre, hospice or home for the elderly.
- ♦ Wherever people are dying, it will bring you powerfully into the present moment.

THE POWER OF GRATITUDE

- ♦ Life begins with an inbreath and ends with an outbreath. Appreciate your breath!
- ♦ Practise expressing gratitude when you wake up in the morning. Say 'thankyou' for whatever inspires you in your life.
- ♦ Practise gratitude before you eat and sleep.
- ♦ Say 'three things I am grateful for are...' every day.
- ♦ Count your blessings daily. Every day remind yourself of how lucky you are. Make a list of all the miracles in your life. To be able to see, feel, walk, talk, laugh, cry, eat, swim, go to the theatre, play with your children... The list will be endless.

THE POWER OF GENEROSITY

♦ Spend a day with a committment to make at least three spontaneous acts of generosity. Look for opportunities to give. When the moments present themselves - go for it!
♦ Do not let a day go by without giving something to somebody. You will find that the opportunities to give will always be there.
♦ Whenever you receive something, make sure you give back more.

The POWER of your PERSONAL DREAMS

Try this for a week or a month:

♦ Visualise as often as you can that your greatest dream in life has come true and surely in time it will.
♦ Think about something you would like to achieve.
♦ Think about the kind of person or personality you would like to be. Spend time every day creating these images, especially before you sleep and just after waking.
♦ See yourself succeeding and achieving your goal.
♦ Imagine you are the person you most admire. Feel what it is like to be that person. How do they think, feel and interact with others?

AT A GLANCE

EQUATION FOR SUCCESS
FIVE STEPS TO SELF-EMPOWERMENT

1   Have a personal commitment to **change** - this may involve taking a risk and trusting. Remember this: small commitment - small result.

2   Utilise the power of the **here and now** and recognise the factors that take you away from it:

- condemning people unnecessarily
- worrying about the past and the future
- fighting the flow of your life

3   Stay in the moment, give your best to it and a tremendous energy and power will start to gently overflow from within you.

4   Discover the power of **gratitude** - a grateful heart under-stands the qualities of sharing and giving. Be grateful for everything in your life - all the people, things and events, whether you label them good or bad. Gratitude enables you to only see the best in every situation and to learn to appreciate the small things in life.

5   Discover the incredible power of **generosity** - one of the most powerful tools for self-growth and one of the key factors in making your life a success. Take part in the energy of life that is circulating naturally - give some money away to a worthy cause!

6   Actualise your dreams - discover their power. Everything you project out actually comes to be. Utilise the power of the subconscious mind. Imagination is more important than knowledge.

PRACTICAL PEACE EXERCISES

AFTERWORD

**'The means may be likened to a seed, the end to a tree,
and there is just the same inviolable connection
between the means and the end
as there is between the seed and the tree.'**

Mahatma Gandhi

The Peace Formula is one very positive offering to drop into the ocean of life. Its ripples can have far-reaching effects because it contains all the secrets you need to know in order to find your own inner harmony. Anyone who studies and lives by this formula will find their life becoming increasingly successful and harmonious. Why? Because it is based on deep spiritual principles that *really work*. The ripples that this one peace-filled pebble will create must inevitably continue to expand and affect everything and everyone around us. It is a basic law of life that we cannot separate ourselves from the consequences of our actions.

The theory of chaos tells us that the tiny movement of a butterfly's wings can have a spectacular influence on the weather systems on the other side of the globe. Small changes can have big effects. Whatever we do as individuals carries a consequence in society, and whatever societies do affects the world. We cannot truly enjoy 'personal peace' without the deepest concern for the world in which we are living. Just as we can add to the pain and suffering on the planet through neglecting this oneness, we can contribute substantially to its healing through focusing our local efforts on positive global change.

My father had always wanted to leave me with something I could use to carry on Gandhi's vision for global harmony. About two days before he passed away, as I was sitting with him in the early hours of the morning, he said to me, 'Mansukh, I have seven sacred seeds to give you that have lain dormant for a long time. And remember,' he said mysteriously, 'it is said in our tradition that when you hold a seed in your hand, you hold the whole tree. I would like you to bring them to life so that future generations will be able to survive by eating the fruits of these trees. Please become a torch bearer for others to walk by your side.' He explained that these laws had been a part of Gandhi's dream for social success.

By the beginning of 1948 Gandhi had worked the principles out in detail and was ready to start implementing them on a mass scale. Everything was in place to begin the process. He had called a meeting of all his closest followers or *satyagrahis* from throughout India to help him formulate the practical means to put them into operation. It was only two weeks before the meeting was due to take place, however, that Gandhi came face to face with Maturan Godse as he walked to his evening prayer meeting. Godse broke through the crowd and bent down in an attitude of reverence before producing a gun from the folds of his robe and shooting four or five bullets into Gandhi's heart. As he fell to the ground Gandhi blessed Godse - and died.

But Gandhi's vision did not die with him. His main message was that we each have the power to control our own destiny and the following seven principles are the means by which we can each take control of the direction in which our society is moving. **The Seven Laws for Social Success** contain the vital link that will help us all to connect our own inner harmony to the whole and it is my great pleasure to introduce you to these principles.

The decisions for affecting global harmony, and therefore the future of the human race, will not be made by politicians or governments, but rather by the thousands of different human interactions we make with each other every day. Everything we do from morning till night has a direct bearing on this global unfolding. Every smile, every kind word, loving touch and moral decision contributes to the harmony of the world we live in. This means we each bear a great responsiblity - for we hold the destiny of our planet and its people in our own hands. It is up to us to take the positive, pro-active steps that will affect that destiny. And it is up to us to take the first step.

GANDHI'S SEVEN LAWS for SOCIAL SUCCESS

Pleasure with Wisdom

Our whole society is based on people fulfilling their desires in the pursuit of pleasure. It is also based on creating more and more desires. I once heard of an advertising manager who proudly declared that his life's purpose was to make everyone in society discontented with who they are and what they have. Can you imagine spending all your time devising ways to make everyone in the country unhappy? And unhappiness is the result of pleasure without wisdom.

The entertainment industry is one of the most significant influences on our thinking today. Entertainment that is designed to inspire and uplift promotes empowered and intelligent people who can think for themselves and shape their own destiny. Used unwisely, the entertainment industry can promote an attitude in which violence and corruption are acceptable. It is up to us to demand TV programmes, films, books and magazines which are wholesome, inspiring and full of hope. If we can promote and encourage pleasures that benefit us all individually and collectively we will definitely be able to reshape the consciousness of society.

Mansukh walking with his son Krishna and 800 people through Rotterdam
to unveil the first Eurowalk Peace Pole in the Netherlands.

Knowledge with Character

Gandhi talked about 'knowledge without character'. He was referring to our ability to ignore what we know to be harmful to ourselves and everyone else. We all know, for instance, that cars pollute the air we breathe, but how many people are prepared to cut down the use of their vehicle - even if not doing so means that their children will suffer in the future? We pollute the soil with herbicides and fertilizers in order to produce more and more food that is denatured. We may smoke knowing we are endangering our health and overstretch ourselves at work to earn more and more money, even though it is becoming apparent that it isn't making us happy. We finish up completely unable to disentangle ourselves from the situation we have created as a result of giving in to that initial desireful thought. To Gandhi it was obvious that it is up to the individual to reverse the situation. Even one person acting with integrity can make an enormous impact. The Nobel Peace Prize winner, Frederick Josef Rotblat, was the first man to have the idea for the atomic bomb. It came to him while he was working in the UK soon after the start of World War II. The way he dealt with this is a perfect example of knowledge with character.

He was so appalled by the idea that he kept quiet about it for over a year in the hope that his silence would prevent the bomb from ever being made. During this time he became increasingly worried in case Hitler should also develop the atom bomb. Eventually, knowing that the

only way Hitler could be prevented from using the bomb would be for the allies to have one first, he explained his idea to the allied military. Rotblat joined the Manhattan project and was instrumental in developing the physics of the bomb, all the time wishing that such a device should never be made. On the day he learned from intelligence sources that Hitler had abandoned the bomb as too difficult he walked out of the Manhattan project, knowing that he would be branded as a traitor and his career ruined.

For nearly a decade Rotblat was shunned by his field, but eventually built up a new career in medical physics leading to stunning advances that created many of the diagnostic machines used in hospitals around the world today. He never gave up his idea for peace and was instrumental in bringing Russian and American scientists together to search for ways to end the cold war. In simple terms, our great knowledge, applied without character, has the power to destroy the world. With character, it has the power to heal the world.

'The final forming of a person's character lies in their own hands.'

Anne Frank

Wealth through Work

Gandhi had a vision of a world in which everyone was self-supporting and self-reliant. Our get-rich-quick society values gaining wealth without effort but the result of this is that more value is being placed on greed than on need.

What are some of the ways we can gain wealth without effort? Inheritance, gambling, exploitation, dishonesty, crime and corruption. Every one of these lead people away from a state of self-sufficiency and self-reliance and a sense of valuing themselves and the people around them. If we have not worked for our wealth we will not value our own efforts and if we exploit others, we are not valuing them. In our modern world of high-powered advertising and credit card consumerism we have created an environment in which we tend to expect instant gratification of our desires without putting in the necessary effort to create the wealth beforehand. This attitude can only lead to discontent, because where there is little effort there will be little satisfaction. When we are standing on our own total efforts, however, we will find that at the end of the day we feel fulfilled and satisfied by our achievements. When we can find deep satisfaction in doing even the smallest of jobs we will lose the idea of wanting to exploit people and the earth because the real reward of work is not financial. Our reward lies in the love of the work itself and the satisfaction of living in an harmonious and connected way with those around us. As Gandhi said, 'Full effort is full victory'.

Politics with Principles

What made Gandhi such a great politician was his ability to relate equally to everyone from the richest to the poorest. This was his power. He made every person feel empowered and renewed in strength by his interaction with them. Politicians with principles are trusted by their electorate to look after the best interests of the people and to withstand the temptation to exploit others.

If you have ever been exploited by someone you will never forget the pain of it. Politicians without principles lose the trust of their electorate. The people then lose interest in the political process and end by becoming indifferent to the future direction of their society.

A society in which people no longer actively participate in their future is on a slow road to disaster. There is a well known saying, 'Where there is no vision the people perish'. Principles in politics enable the whole of society to regain its vision and is a way of recreating our harmonious future.

'Behind every noble life there are principles that have fashioned it.'
David Lorimer

Worship with Giving

What is worship? Our need to worship comes from a deep and intrinsic longing to touch the very highest part of ourselves. Real worship is charged with sincerity, enthusiasm and aspiration together with an outpouring of unconditional love. The fact that many of the wars on this planet have involved religious differences indicates very clearly that there may not be many people experiencing genuine worship. It is not religion that is responsible, however, but rather worship without giving.

St Francis captured the essence of worship in his famous prayer when he said, 'It is in giving that we receive.' The world today seems to be advocating another prayer: 'It is in taking that we receive.' Self-seeking automatically closes us off from the highest, most divine part of ourselves and this creates a very deep pain within us. How sad it is that people have forgotten this simple law of life. It actually contains the secret to everything they are looking for. In their desperate search for love people have forgotten how to love and an inability to love is the root cause of suffering and spiritual deprivation.

If we could just decide to make giving a priority in our daily interactions everything we do could become an act of worship and a means to connect to the very highest within us. Our greatest wealth, therefore, lies in our capacity to experience worship in giving, loving and thinking of others' needs before our own.

When we can truly love one another, God will become a living reality for each one of us.

Over 1,500 people gathered to welcome the peace flame at St Lauren's Church, which was bombed during the war and is now a symbol of the phoenix rising.

Science with Humanity

Science is the tool by which humanity explores its place in the universe. My professor at university used to say, 'Science is the discovery of truth'. As such, it is supposed to give us the means for making our lives more harmonious and intimately connected with the flow of life around us. At its best, science gives us the tools to achieve the health and comfort necessary to fully explore the human quest for happiness and fulfilment.

At its worst, science can access knowledge which, if abused, could be responsible for the destruction of life on earth. More and more commonly science is used to take us into a technological world where we may end up living in tiny rooms in which we become de-natured and disconnected from each other and therefore from the natural flow of life. Science in this form contributes to isolation and separation and this breeds fear between people and nations. Our humanity rebels at the thought.

> **'Science sometimes runs the risk of not seeing the truth, because it does not want to know about miracles.'**
>
> *Jacques Cousteau*

The UN has calculated that every human being could be given enough food, shelter, sanitation and education to live comfortably for no more than the money spent annually on golf and only one thirteenth of what is spent on cigarettes. Just imagine if science were to be diverted from supporting military destruction to methods of living in harmony with our planet. We do have the power as individuals to influence such a move, because it is we who decide which projects are funded. We are each responsible for the supply and demand which dictates them through the things we buy. Many scientists like Einstein heard the call of humanity and altered the course of science's contribution to the evolution of peace.

As Eknath Easwaran once said, 'We have never before had more cars and machines to save time, but we have also never before had to spend two to three hours a day commuting in a car filled with toxic fumes. We have never before had such excellent medical equipment, but neither have we had such pollution to endanger our health. We have never before had nuclear power and never before have we had nuclear accidents.' We really do have the power to shape the world of technology. Science is serving our wants and needs which means that if we each decide to simplify those needs we can direct our technology towards healing and restoring the earth.

Commerce without Morality

The driving force behind commerce is that we all strive to be successful and to have all that we want to achieve happiness. But if our business dealings are based on greed and exploitation rather than helping people to live successfully and happily the result can only be suffering for everyone concerned. Happiness that is built on the suffering of others can never last because outer exploitation leads to inner deprivation.

We human beings are the only creatures on the earth that take more than they need. The emerging crisis is that people and their human dignity are becoming less important than producing goods to sell in order to make more and more money. The temptation to sell more instant and fragile products at cheaper prices can easily go beyond healthy competition to exploitation of all the people involved. The buying and selling of goods to make profit at every step ultimately leads to a greed which eliminates any benefit to the human being. And if we are not careful mechanisation could eliminate the human resource altogether. The reward for businessmen and women working at fever pitch in the high pressure world of commerce is not always success and wealth. It is often cancer, heart disease, breakdown and depression.

Is it really worth it?

We are not all helpless victims of this commercial madness, for we hold the power to change things in our own hands. At the time of writing this I received a letter from a large food company in which they described a major shift in policy as a result of letters they had received from the public. We really can make a difference. We can each take time to find out which companies promote fairness and which ones contribute to inequality. We can reject the greed and exploitation of certain companies by refusing to buy their goods. We can also support initiatives based on a philosophy of caring for people and the environment.

**'There's enough in the world for everyone's need,
but not for everyone's greed.'**
Mahatma Gandhi

In Conclusion

Once these seeds of clarity and real fulfilment have been sown in our minds, each one of us must contemplate deeply upon the living truths they contain. They are at the same time practical, essential and an absolute necessity for our present and our future. Although Gandhi's dying words, as he fell to the ground were 'Bless you', the responsibility lies with us to turn that blessing into a formidable force which can shape our destiny and the destiny of our children.

As we draw near to the end of this millenium, we prepare to enter a new phase in the history of our humanity. And as the human family becomes more acutely aware of the fragility of its survival, there has never been a time more suited to reviewing where we are heading.

The effort that we need to make has now been considerably reduced because the answers have been given to us. We should be delighted and excited about the great possibility this presents. As Gandhi said, 'Those people who say that politics and religion do not mix, do not know what religion is about.' Similarly, I would like to say that human spirituality and religion involves our interaction with each and every one of these seven spiritual principles.

Half a century has passed since that noble figure collapsed onto the ground, but his vision lives on. Now is the time to pick up the torch which symbolises the flame of our own vision and commitment and to walk on together.

ABOUT THE AUTHOR

B orn in Kenya in the fifties, Mansukh Patel was faced in his early life with a whole gamut of experiences. He lived through the Mau Mau uprising right on his doorstep and faced many personal struggles arising from poverty and isolation. At the opposite end of the spectrum he developed a close communion with the animal kingdom and the world of nature to which he was always able to turn for support. From a very early age, he dedicated himself to his own intensive training programme in the fields of yoga, meditation and the expansion of the inner dimension. All this has created a being of great sensitivity, with a real understanding of human struggles and suffering and a deep yearning to be of service to humanity. It is here that we have the basis for his present philosophy of which he says, 'May we accept from each other that which we need, and give to others that which is precious to us.'

At the age of twelve he said goodbye to the country of his birth, leaving behind the challenging yet simple outdoor life of his early years, to be greeted by an English winter and the complexities of a technological society. In England his thirst for knowledge took a new turn as he embraced the world of science - just one more aspect of his search for truth. He achieved high merit in his studies at university under the guidance of Professor WC Evans F.R.S., making an outstanding contribution to the fields of oncology and cancer research.

His profound knowledge of the relationship between body and mind inspired him to teach others how the two work in unison. He started to teach his own unique style of therapeutic yoga twenty years ago. Since then he has taught yoga, health and philosophy to thousands of people across the globe, travelling from the Far East across India, Tibet, Europe, America and Australasia. He has developed a reputation of being a teacher who has the potential and capability to inspire and uplift people from all walks of life, from very simple people to those in positions of high responsibility.

Mansukh's unique contribution to our lives lies in the way he has highlighted the essential unity between the parapsychological aspects of western thought and the ancient infallible principles of the eastern masters. This visionary synthesis of complementary thought has provided a platform of growth for many, many people.

144

Mansukh's insight into the nature of the human condition is deep and penetrating. His logical and human approach sometimes seems too simple, but as he himself says, 'Truth is simple. It is so simple that it escapes us.' His calm, gentle presence and simple philosophy seem to take the harshness out of life, so that as challenges come to us we are able to see them in a clear light and accept them all with a sense of calmness.

A man with a vision, all of Mansukh's time and energy is now completely dedicated to bringing peace to individuals in all parts of the world. To this end, he and his colleagues from the Life Foundation have created a world-wide network of centres from which people of vision constantly work to support the cause of peace. He is always on the move as Eurowalk 2000 travels across the globe, taking simple self-help and de-traumatisation techniques into areas of conflict. He has always maintained that when we are no longer divided within ourselves, we will find peace entering our lives. When we no longer see distinctions between people, there will be peace in the world.

Please read his words with an open heart and an open mind - because as he says, 'If we are to bring peace into this world, someone has to start. Please let it be you.'

How can you refuse such a call?

LIFE FOUNDATION WORLDWIDE

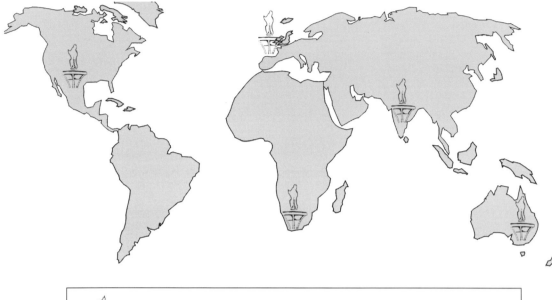

Teams of people are now working in America, Australia, India, N.Ireland, the Netherlands, Germany as well as throughout the UK.

We are a group of professional therapists from a wide range of backgrounds, dedicated to developing the highest potential in people. Our work was first formalised in the UK in 1988 with the formation of the Life Foundation School of Therapeutics (LFST), our not-for-personal-profit trading company. Life Foundation International was formed in 1998 to carry on the charitable work of LFST as a result of a tremendous interest and expansion of our work in war and disaster zones.

Life Foundation International (LFI) specialises in taking de-traumatisation techniques into areas of conflict and trauma. LFI uses a unique Body Heart Mind (BHM) approach to overcoming emotional pain. BHM techniques have now been taken into every continent and successfully applied to help refugees and aid workers as well as ordinary people in nearly every sphere of life.

The Life Foundation School of Therapeutics's international peace initiative Eurowalk 2000 works both globally and locally, teaching these techniques around the world. Eurowalk originally evolved out of the world peace journey FWF (Friendship without Frontiers), which taught BHM in 31 countries over a period of 18 months.

146

1992/93

Friendship Without Frontiers. LFST members undertook an eighteen month world-wide journey to teach BHM techniques in over 30 countries and take part in the Earth Summit in Rio, Brazil.

1994

Lifewalk 2000. Teams of therapists and teachers set out to walk and teach across the UK. Life Aid supplied 2000 boxes of food and medical supplies to emergency medical staff and refugees in Bosnia.

1995

Inauguration of Eurowalk 2000. Teams supported three stages of the Nipponzan Myohoji peace walk from Auschwitz to Hiroshima. Eurowalk 2000 team walked and taught from Auschwitz to the UK. LifeAid sent approximately 5 tonnes of food, clothing and medical aid to Bosnia and Croatia. LFST received the Gordon Wilson Peace Award. Eurowalk 2000 toured Ireland North and South to train cross-community workers in BHM de-traumatisation techniques.

1996

Eurowalk 2000 teams visited former Yugoslavia to train counsellors of the UNHCR, the Red Cross, the Medical Centre for Human Rights and the Croatian Association of Psychotherapists in self-help techniques for healing war-time trauma. Training was also given to NGO groups and in refugee camps. LifeAid sent 7 tonnes of food supplies to former Yugoslavia.

1997

Eurowalk 2000 walked and taught BHM techniques across the length and breadth of the UK.

1998

Eurowalk 2000 Russia taught Russian and Chechen child psychologists in a North Caucausus Training programme. A nation-wide shoe collection was organised by LFST for children in Moldova. 6,000 pairs were collected. LFST trainers taught detraumatisation techniques to government officials in Kathmandu, Nepal and members of the All Party Parliamentary Group for Peace and Reconciliation in the House of Lords, London.

1999

LFST teams taught detraumatisation techniques to UNHCR representatives in Dacca, Bangladesh and conflict-torn areas of South Africa and South Sudan with additional programmes in Kenya. LFST organised a nation-wide collection of 3,000 hand tools, 200 sewing machines and 50 bicycles as charity aid for Africa, providing over 16,000 people with the means to become self-sufficient. Emergency humanitarian aid from the UK and the Netherlands included shipments of 47 tonnes of food aid for Kosovo, shoe box collections for refugee children in the UK and peace vigils in the UK, the Netherlands, Germany and the USA. The Peace Pole project was started with Peace Poles in the UK, the Netherlands and the USA. The Life Peace Prayer Project was initiated in the USA. 1999 also saw the commencement of the Life Youth Project, which trains outstanding young people world-wide to be peace-makers. LFI organised a major peace walk, attended by nearly 1000 people in Rotterdam, in the Netherlands. LFI initiated BHM detraumatisation programmes in Peace and Reconciliation centres across Belfast, Northern Ireland and in Nairobi, Kenya for refugees from Rwanda, Burundi, the Congo and Angola.

WHAT PEOPLE SAY ABOUT THE PEACE FORMULA

'The process of examining one's own emotions can be quite daunting and beset by so many pitfalls, so much so that it is often easier to brush it aside. With the wisdom and guidance of this book, however, I have been able to do this fruitfully and thereby have a clearer perspective of myself and my life. The reward of taking the plunge into self examination is that I can now stand beside my fellow human beings and help them more sympathetically.'

Dr Allan Forsyth – General Practitioner

'I am so very grateful to Mansukh Patel for this amazing book. I have read and worked with it for years and it has shown me in many different ways how to recognise who I am and why I am here. It has shown me how to be happier and be at peace with myself. It has given me self esteem and inspired me to recognise the good and God in everything and everyone. Working with The Peace Formula in a group has shown me my life's purpose and yes, it has changed my life.'

Elspeth Johnson – Dru Yoga Teacher

'There is no journey more exciting than the inner journey, no discovery more revealing than the inner discovery, no challenge more rewarding or of greater value than the process of inner growth. I have found that The Peace Formula really is a practical and every day guide for personal happiness and fulfilment.'

Peter Legge – University Lecturer

'I carry this book everywhere I go because it is so invaluable and has practical techniques that anyone can use to discover peace and tranquillity within the home and workplace. I have run a ten week course with a group of friends and have also used it as a busy motber of two children to bring balance and harmony back into my own life.'

Sylvia Bell – Housewife

'This book really works!'

Dr David Barry – Scientist and Theoretical Physicist

'I have been running a Peace Formula group for many years now and have found that the lessons and exercises have been so effective. They have made a significant difference to the people in the group. One trained counsellor who had been working with children told me that the difference between a Peace Formula workshop and any other she had been to was that she came away knowing that she had changed, not just hoping. If you want something to take you a long way fast, then use the Peace Formula!'

Sue Lightfoot – Peace Formula Group Leader

'Thank you for this beautiful instrument upon which I am learning to play a better tune within myself.'

Mary Compton-Rickett – Lawyer

By the Same Author

THE DANCE BETWEEN JOY AND PAIN
Dr Mansukh Patel and Rita Goswami

This pocket handbook has become a source of inspiration and reference for thousands of people since it was first published in 1995. It is a manual for mastering all the negative emotions we experience, from anger and jealousy to loneliness and grief. Practical movements, breathing exercises and hand gestures combine to transform emotions into positive tools to enrich every aspect of life. Now in its fifth reprint, 'The Dance Between Joy and Pain' is also available in Dutch, French and German.

FACE TO FACE WITH LIFE
Dr Mansukh Patel and John Jones

This is a powerful handbook for successful living...it is also a miraculous true story. Enjoy the gripping story of a group of University students who became the pioneers of the Life Foundation, and who have brought real happiness into thousands of lives world-wide. This popular book contains over a hundred ground-breaking techniques to increase self-esteem, improve relationships and develop inner calm and is now available in Dutch from Ankh Hermes.

CRISIS AND THE MIRACLE OF LOVE
Dr Mansukh Patel and Dr Helena Waters

At every stage of life, there is a point of power, a potent time when an intense amount of energy is made available to us for our emotional and spiritual growth. This book reveals how to access your creative potential at your stage of life, giving fascinating insights into every conceivable challenge you are likely to meet in your life. If you want to know how to turn crisis into opportunity, to create successful, lasting relationships and understand your children and learn from them, this book tells you how.

OPENING TO MIRACLES *Sally Langford and Jane Patel*

This uplifting music cassette is based on the Peace Formula's Five Steps for Self-Empowerment. Sally and Jane have created a unique collection of vibrant songs which use rhythm and guitars to bring affirmations to life. Positivity and self-empowerment will fill you as you listen to this transforming tape.

To order any of these products, please contact Snowdon Lodge: 01248 602900

MEDITATION CORRESPONDENCE COURSE
Dr Mansukh Patel and Pam McGregor

For over five years this correspondence course has been successfully bringing inner calm and balance to people in the UK and overseas. This meditation foundation course will help both beginners and experienced practitioners. As a day-by-day guide you can advance from basic introductory skills to become a seasoned meditator. You will receive 24 monthly packages and 6 supplementary audio tapes. The course can be started at any time of the year.

WALKING WITH THE BHAGAVAD GITA
(Vol. 1) *Savitri MacCuish, Dr Mansukh Patel and John Jones*

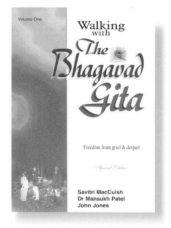

In this beautiful book, Mansukh Patel magnificently portrays the dialogue between Lord Krishna and Arjuna in a way that is both exciting and deeply moving. The inspired commentary by Savitri MacCuish and John Jones, includes ways to apply the Gita's message to your daily life. The heart of the Gita is conveyed in a way never before encountered. This edition is the first volume of Walking with the Bhagavad Gita, and covers chapters 1-6. This is a book to treasure for the rest of your life.

THE BHAGAVAD GITA VIDEO SERIES   *narrated by*
Dr Mansukh Patel

In this series of stunning documentaries, one for each chapter of the Bhagavad Gita, Mansukh's original insights into its message are illustrated by fascinating anecdotes from his own life and his experiences on Eurowalk 2000. Mansukh also demonstrates flowing Dru Yoga movements which complement the Gita's message. This series of films has been shown on Dutch national TV. Please enquire about which films are currently available as they are being released on a regular basis.

ACKNOWLEDGEMENTS

This book has come into existence thanks to the help of many dear friends. I would like to offer my gratitude to all the team members of Eurowalk 2000 as well as all the inspiring people we have met during our numerous travels for supporting our work worldwide.

As always, my deepest love and gratitude to my wife, Radhika, and our three beautiful children, Arjuna, Krishna and Radha, whose unending support for my work and vision make everything possible. My special thanks to Sally Langford for compiling my words and Jane Clapham for her layout, cover design and photography. I would also like to thank Craig Robertson for his photography and help with graphics, Elna Obreen for the Eurowalk photography and Bart Verstraete for his photographs of our Rotterdam Peace Walk. Other photographers I would like to thank are John Scard, Gordon Turner, John Jones, Jeff Cushing, Philip Englelen, Peter Gates and Shona Sutherland.

My heart-felt gratitude to Robert Muller for his visionary poem. I would also like to thank Savitri MacCuish, Andrew Wells and Chris Barrington for their wise and very valuable contributions, and a special mention to Chris Hunter from the Centre for Peacemaking and Community Development in London and Moscow. My gratitude also goes to the proof-readers Ruth Boaler, Margaret Nicholas, Denise Reagan, Annette Crisswell and Jess Scard. Finally I would like to offer my gratitude to Kate Couldwell, Barbara Wood and Gordon Turner for their endless loving support.

TO CONTACT US

The Life Foundation School of Therapeutics has established the following permanent bases:

Life Foundation School of Therapeutics(UK)
Registered Office
Maristowe House
Dover Street, Bilston
West Midlands WV14 6AL
Tel: 01902 409164
Fax: 01902 497362
E-mail: info@lifefoundation.org.uk

Life Foundation School of Therapeutics(UK)
International Training Centre
Snowdon Lodge
Nant Ffrancon
Ty'n y Maes
Bethesda
Gwynedd LL57 3LX
Tel: 01248 602900
Fax: 01248 602004
E-mail: snowdonlodge@lifefoundation.org.uk

The Life Foundation School of Therapeutics, U.S.A.
5004 Sunsuite Trail South
Colorado Springs
CO 80917
USA
Tel: 719 - 574 5452
Fax: 719 - 597 7929
E-mail: reggiedoe@aol.com

Life Foundation School of Therapeutics (Netherlands)
Postbus 88
6670 AB ZETTEN
The Netherlands
Tel: 488 - 491387
Fax: 488 - 491545
E-mail: lfstnether@aol.com

Life Foundation School of Therapeutics (Australia) Ltd
PO Box 543
Southport BC
Queensland 4215
Australia
E-mail: lifeaus@aol.com

There are also full-time LFST representatives in the following areas:
UK - London, Newcastle, Edinburgh and Belfast, Germany - Dortmund.
For details of events in these areas please contact the Outreach Director, Life Foundation School of Therapeutics(UK), Snowdon Lodge (see above).